CRETE WAS MY WATERLOO

The author, 1940

CRETE WAS MY WATERLOO

NEVILLE CHESTERTON

*A true eyewitness account of the sinking of
the Lancastria, the Battle of Crete and
P.O.W. Experiences 1940–45*

JANUS PUBLISHING COMPANY
London, England

First published in Great Britain 1995
by Janus Publishing Company
Edinburgh House, 19 Nassau Street
London W1N 7RE

British Library Cataloguing-in-Publication Data.
A catalogue record for this book is available
from the British Library.

ISBN 1 85756 198 8

Cover design Harold King

Printed & bound in England by
Antony Rowe Ltd, Chippenham, Wiltshire

To my wife Margaret.
For her help & encouragement.

Foreword

Many books have been written about the wartime exploits of great heroism and daring by officers in the various services, but very few ordinary lower-ranking servicemen have thought their experiences worthy of putting on record.

My wife once remarked that it would have been interesting to have had the true life eyewitness account of the Battle of Agincourt by one of the ordinary archers, or the true story of an infantryman at Waterloo, or a lower-deck sailor at Trafalgar. This made me wonder if my own unheroic wartime experiences might not be of interest to some people. 'They also serve who only stand and wait,' said Milton.

Countless ordinary lives were completely altered and disrupted by the actions of a lowly corporal in the Second World War, and thousands of people who would be classed as 'also-rans' tried to do their bit to help their country protect its proud heritage. Many lost their lives; their stories will never be known. We were all like pawns being moved about in a giant game of chess over which we had no control.

It is sad to think that the majority of the present generation neither know or care about the terrible events which the older generation (now termed 'wrinklies' if still living) had to face. The sinking of the *Lancastria* was the greatest sea disaster ever known, greater than the sinking of the *Titanic* or *Lusitania* and yet the schoolchildren of today probably have never heard of it.

It is also surprising to think that the British participants in the Crete campaign are not allowed to have a medal, whereas the Australians and New Zealanders were given them.

The German POWs were granted pensions by their government at the end of the war, but our POWs, even those poor souls in Japanese hands, had nothing, thanks to some twit in our government saying 'our own men will be well provided for,' and then proceeded to forget them.

Nearly all the survivors of the prison camps have some type of disability caused by the privations of war, some proven injuries, others mental from delayed stress, but there are no large payouts for the POW 'wrinklies' like the present scandalous payout of huge sums being given to women who get pregnant in the Services!

These are the days when footballers burst into tears when they kick a ball the wrong way, or have a grievance – what a contrast to those who, knowing they were trapped like rats in the hold of the sinking *Lancastria*, were heard to be singing 'Roll out the Barrel' as the ship went down.

It is to these unsung, unknown, ordinary people that I dedicate my humble record of wartime memories.

N R Chesterton (ex-REs and POW)

Chapter One

My unexciting, uneventful and peaceful life as a junior railway clerk was given a sudden jolt by Fate when Hitler began his warlike manoeuvres in Europe and laughed at poor innocent Mr Chamberlain's peace proposals.

I thought they must have been scraping the barrel when I was suddenly called up and conscripted into the army at the age of nineteen, in January 1940. I had never been away from home before, having lived all my life in Wednesbury, Staffordshire, an ancient town which had turned industrial in the nineteenth century and was now almost a continuation of the outskirts of Birmingham. It was rather sooty and dreary, like so many of the West Midlands towns which were termed the Black Country.

First of all, at very short notice, I was posted to Derby, where I was billeted in a private house with another budding soldier. As I had worked on the railway, although in a clerical position, I was drafted into the Royal Engineers, and later was put into a unit called 'Movement Control'. We were told we were a 'Special' unit but, on looking back, I wonder who thought that up.

When I had first picked up my uniform and rifle, and was on my way back to my digs, an officer passed me, and as I had been told you always salute an officer, I proudly did so – with a cigarette in my mouth and my rifle held upside-down. He turned a face of wrath on me and called me every name he could think of, which brought me sharply up-to-date with the latest army vocabulary. As this was right in the centre of Derby and there were crowds of people around, there were quite a few interested spectators who sniggered to themselves and must have thought, 'What the hell have we got to protect us!'

In the centre of Derby I remember seeing a lot of black canisters left on pavements and streets and I wondered what they were for. It appeared that when an air-raid warning sounded they were lit up and gave off clouds of smoke to form a smokescreen. There was sometimes a pall of smoke over the city but it did not stop it from being bombed quite badly at times.

Incidentally, I happened to be wearing brown shoes instead of the regulation army boots, so was stopped by every MP and officer and rebuked for slovenly appearance, but I did have a good excuse and a doctor's certificate for this, having had a deep burn just below my ankle. This had been caused when I had been in hospital some months previously to have my tonsils out, and a nurse had carelessly left an unwrapped hot water bottle touching my ankle which had burned it badly, and it had not properly healed up.

We were then given some basic training with rifle practice, lectures about troop movements and the running of the railways and, later in the month, I was sent off to Grimsby to work in the Railway Traffic (RTO) office.

I was placed in a private billet with two other men, and found we had to sleep three in a bed. What would they think about that these days? One was snoring and kicking all night, he must have been a footballer, and it wasn't very comfortable. Luckily most of my time was spent on night duty.

I always seemed to be on duty at night, about 8 pm to 9 am next day. There was a large number of troops passing through and I was supposed to put them on the right track, issue warrants, etc. My landlady, who was very kind, must have thought I needed feeding up, as she fed me both day and night. I found the sandwiches she had provided far too much for myself but could always find a hungry soldier to give them to.

One of my duties was to keep in touch with what I called the Ghost Train – this was an armoured train which was travelling

2

around in the area. Messages were received of its whereabouts, but I never saw it.

We were instructed most of the time by two staff sergeants who were regular soldiers. We used to call them Tweedledum and Tweedledee. We hated the sight of them, as they were right toadies to the officers, but treated us like imbeciles. They were like twins and were always together. They marched everywhere in step, wearing their red sashes and looking like something out of a Gilbert and Sullivan operetta. Whatever one said, the other would back him up. With their buttons and cap badges shining, trousers pressed to knife edges and shoes polished, they expected us to look the same. No officer within a hundred yards could possibly miss their over-smart salute. There is an army phrase for this kind of person, but I won't use it here.

I met a very nice girl in Grimsby whose name was Mona. I only met her three times, and kissed her only once, that's how it was in those days. She wrote me a letter almost every week when later I was a POW and I shall never forget her kindness. I only saw her once after the war. She had joined the WAAF as an aircraft controller and found another boyfriend in the RAF whom she married.

My mother used to write to me fairly frequently, but my brother, due to health reasons, was in a reserved occupation.

After some weeks I was recalled to Derby and made up to lance-corporal; this was my first and last promotion.

After my spell in Derby, our unit was divided into two, one to go to Norway and the other to France, and I was in the latter. We were marched off to the station and to my surprise people were lining the streets and cheering to give us a good send-off. We all had our large packs on our backs and small valises on our sides, with gas masks on our chests, and were also carrying our kitbags. How I got down to the station I shall never know, I think I dragged my kitbag most of the way. I certainly did not feel like any sort of hero!

Standing at the end of the platform were Tweedledum and Tweedledee, smartly saluting, with smirks on their faces. I expect they were thinking, 'Those poor sods are going abroad, whilst we are staying here having a good time!'

We then travelled down to Dover and were put on a cross-Channel steamer bound for Cherbourg. It was overnight, and very few could find anywhere to have a sleep as it was very overcrowded but, thank goodness, the sea was quite calm.

Chapter Two

On arriving in France, we were put into box-wagons, and travelled to various places. France seemed to be very flat and uninteresting to me. We seemed to be going around in circles; in fact, I don't think anyone knew where we were going or what we were supposed to do.

We eventually finished up about thirty miles from the port of St Nazaire on the Bay of Biscay, and set up camp in a field not far from a village. There were about fifty of us altogether, the rest of our unit having gone to Norway.

For a time we did some more training and rifle practice, I actually hit the target once or twice. We did guard duties, etc, and I remember thinking, This is a most peculiar war, nothing seems to be happening.

After a few weeks of this inactivity we began to get some very bad news of the state of the war, and heard that the Germans were breaking through on all fronts. A disturbing rumour came in that there was a big evacuation of our army from another part of France – but we never heard the word Dunkirk. German planes were flying over fairly high but we never saw any British planes. We didn't know where the German planes were heading; later we were to find out, much to our cost. We didn't realise it, but we were about to be thrown into the real war in no uncertain way.

One evening, when it seemed quiet, I said to my pal, 'Come on, let's try and get to the village and see what's going on there.' We trudged off and got to a small town where there appeared to be a cinema. We decided to go in and see the film, although we wouldn't be able to understand much of it as it would be all in French, but at least it would be something to look at away from the camp. We went in free, as there seemed to be no customers about and it seemed very quiet. There were not more than half a dozen people in there with us.

There seemed to be quite a lot of excited chatter going on, which of course we could not understand, and the cinema gradually began to empty. By the end of the film I said to my friend, 'There's something funny going on here, where has everybody gone? They've all cleared off – we're the only ones in here!'

When we got outside, we found the whole place seemed to be deserted, so we made our way back to the camp as quickly as possible to find out what was going on.

We were greeted by a corporal who said, 'Where the hell have you two been? There's a big panic on and we're going to move out very soon.' It wasn't until the next morning that we were told that France had capitulated and we had to get to the port of St Nazaire as quickly as possible, and find a ship to take us back to England.

We were called on parade next morning and told we would be leaving soon, taking our 'small kit' with us. My friend Derek, who, next to myself, was about the most unsuitable person to be a soldier and who was always in trouble, was outside his tent having a shave. He had his pack on his back, upside-down, and looked to have a bit of a hangover, but to be truthful he always looked like that. The sergeant-major turned red in the face and yelled at him to get a blankety-blank move on, so Derek rushed out on parade with one half of his face shaved and the other lathered. The CSM yelled, 'If there are any more soldiers like you in the British army, then God help us!'

The next thing was a big panic because the captain couldn't find his steel helmet and wouldn't leave without it. Eventually it was found, and we moved off. On thinking back, it was ironic that without these two delays we should probably have lost our lives.

We found three army lorries which had been abandoned and piled on board. Then we found that nobody was able to drive them. We had dispatch riders with us but they had never been trained to drive lorries. After a while they managed to get us moving, jolting and stopping, and at a very slow pace. We gradually made our way to St Nazaire.

As we got nearer the port, we could see columns of fire rising and heard a lot of gunfire. German planes were very active overhead but they were too occupied in attacking the port to bother about us.

I said to the chap next to me in the lorry, 'It looks as if we shall have a warm welcome,' and we wondered if we would ever get through it and get back to England. Everyone was very tense in the truck.

We arrived at the docks in St Nazaire at last to find a chaotic scene, and we could see that several ships in the harbour had already been hit and were burning.

We left the trucks by the side of the road and made our way down to the jetty. On the left-hand side of this, we noticed that piles of army coats were arranged in single file, with the object of making the planes think this was a line of troops. This ruse seemed to have been successful, as the planes strafed them up and down many times, and this probably saved lives.

We ran along the other side of the jetty in small groups, dodging the bullets and luckily none of us was hit. There was a small French tender alongside the quay, which took half of us on board. It already looked to be full of troops, and we were packed like sardines, ready to be taken out to a British ship a few miles off the quay.

Here I would like to pay a tribute to the captain and crew of the French tender we were on (as well as other brave French sailors) who ran the gauntlet of continual strafing and bombing all the way, carrying their loads of British people out to the big ships outside the harbour.

I kept hearing the plops in the water around us all the way, as the bombs dropped near us, but thankfully we were not hit. It was providential that it was a calm sea as we were so low down in the water; it seemed to be a very small boat to be carrying so many people. We thought the French sailors were so good that we all gave them what cigarettes we had as a small payment.

We were being carried towards a large liner, which was lying at anchor a few miles away. As we got closer to it, we could see that it was already crowded with troops. As we drew alongside, I looked up and saw the name *Lancastria*.

Chapter Three

As we touched the ship, thinking rescue was in sight, an officer came down the gangway to us and shouted, 'You can't come on here, we are too full already, go and find another ship to take you!'

Very disappointed, we pulled away, watched by hundreds of men lining the decks. There were a couple of other ships some distance away and we took a course towards them. At this moment we saw three Spitfires fly over very high up, they were probably hurrying for home, out of ammunition and probably short of fuel.

Before we had gone a hundred yards, a German Dornier bomber flew over us very low and dropped a bomb right on the bridge of the liner *Lancastria*. Almost at once, three more bombs fell onto the ship and we heard the explosions. We watched in horror and utter disbelief, thinking of all the poor souls on board. We heard afterwards that one bomb blew the bridge off the ship, and must have gone right through it. The accommodation below decks was packed full of men who had little or no chance of escaping.

As we watched, the liner started to sink by the bows and it turned over onto its port side before our eyes. Men were sliding into the sea from the starboard side. The sea was covered with oil with hundreds of men jumping overboard into it, which was a horrific sight, but we could not help as we were too far away and our small tender was overfull already.

We realised we were witnessing a very terrible disaster, and that scene remains etched in my memory as if it was yesterday, in all its dreadful detail.

This was my first experience of the horror of war.

Other ships in the area were racing up to help pick up survivors. I did not know the names of the naval ships at that time, but have since learned that one was the destroyer *Highlander*, which saved hundreds of souls (there were many women on board as well as the troops – ATS, Salvation Army, nurses, wives and even children). There was also the armed trawler *Cambridgeshire* which rescued about a thousand survivors.

One story reported afterwards was a civilian man and his wife with their two small babies, who slid into the water holding them up. They held the children up between them until they got parted, and the husband managed to hold the baby between his teeth and swim towards a rescue boat, while the wife held her baby above her head until she was rescued – they were all eventually picked up by the destroyer *Highlander*.

One survivor, now in his eighties and ill in hospital, told a friend how he slid down the side of the ship and, when he hit the water, he was surrounded by hundreds of dead fish and he got covered in oil. He said the planes were still dropping bombs all around them, as well as strafing. As he got into the water he heard those men trapped inside the *Lancastria* singing 'Roll out the Barrel'. After about two hours in the oily water, he was eventually picked up by a French fisherman. When he was pulled out he found he had lost his trousers – there had been quite a lot of money in his trouser pocket and if he had not lost it he would have given it all to the French fisherman. We should be grateful to the French for saving many lives that dreadful day.

Mrs Diane Perryman of Newton Abbot told me that her father, Staff Sergeant Bertie Cook, was on the *Lancastria* when she sank. He could not swim, but had a friend, Paddy (surname unknown), who could, and this man pulled her father up to a floating plank and draped him over it. After some hours, Paddy lost consciousness and slipped off the plank into the water and was lost. Sergeant Cook also lost consciousness after a time, and he was twenty-four hours in the water. When he was picked up by a passing vessel, name unknown, he was completely naked except for his watch, and black with oil. Someone in the ship gave him a polo-necked jumper to put on, and eventually he was brought in to Plymouth. His wife met him on Newton Abbot station, and didn't recognise him – he was still completely black. It took weeks rubbing him with lard to try and get the oil off him. He was always tortured with guilt because his friend, who had saved him, had lost his life, but there was nothing he could possibly have done about it. His daughter said it altered his whole personality, and for years he would not speak about his ordeal.

I am putting this in this record, because so few people have ever heard of the terrible tragedies of so many people who were on the *Lancastria*. People have specifically asked that their reminiscences should be written about, as they have seen nothing about this awful event in print. The people that suffered these horrific events did not get any counselling, as they would get these days, but were sent back into daily life in the army or forces to get on with living as best they could. We have also heard from survivors who had been landed in France, and went around naked and dazed, until someone eventually gave them a few clothes.

An account which I have read later was of a sixty-five-year old army officer, who was on board the *Lancastria* and mounted a Bren gun on the deck of the sinking ship and fired away at the German bombers. He kept on firing until he eventually slid off the deck of the ship as it keeled over. He was not seen again. There were many similar cases of heroism which have never been given publicity.

One survivor, whose memoirs I have been given to read, recorded that he watched from the deck of the *Lancastria* as a German plane, banking steeply, dropped its bombs onto the deck of the liner *Oronsay*, which was lying a short distance to starboard and was the ship that I was eventually taken on board. He saw a shower of debris from the bridge fly in all directions. Mr Joe Sweeney, now living in Canada, gives this graphic account:

Three more hours elapsed before the *Lancastria* had a near

11

miss from a bomb, then another German bomber made another attack on us. The whole ship gave a shudder, which felt ominous and frightening, and then it made a violent lurch to port. We knew then that we had got to get up on deck and would have to try and swim for it, as it was obvious that the ship was now preparing to sink. All the companionways and staircases were choc-a-bloc with troops, many still had their packs and rifles. Then, without warning, the water began to flow down the companion-way. Gradually I made my way with the crowd surging upwards towards a glimmer of light, until we reached one of the lower decks. Seconds later the liner lurched again to port. I could not swim, so I followed others out of the lounge. Chairs, tables, and everything that could float was grabbed and thrown overboard.

I realised now that the ship was sinking fast by the bows, and the stern was slowly rising. Hundreds of heads were bobbing up and down in the water amidst a mass of floating flotsam. Some people were getting hit by the objects thrown overboard, and some men disappeared under the water.

Above the sound of hissing steam escaping from broken boilers and pipes and the clanging of bells we could hear the sound of pom-pom guns from the deck.

I had to get into the water as far as possible from the sinking ship, as I did not want to be sucked under as it made its final plunge. Many of us began to sing popular songs and hymns to try and boost morale.

I took off my footwear and jacket, but did not remove my trousers. I took a running jump over the rail of the ship, but instead of falling into the water I hit the starboard side plates, and slid down onto the propeller shaft, which was then about forty feet out of the water. There were many others with me in various states of undress. Then there was another convulsive shudder and we realised that we had to get into the water, and most of us jumped.

On hitting the water, I seemed to go down interminably, but though I couldn't swim, I held my arms upwards and held my breath for what seemed to be a very long time. When I reached the surface, I tried to float on my back.

People were fighting to stay afloat, grabbing anything and anyone in sight. One man desperately grabbed me, taking me back under, but lost his grip, and I surfaced again.

There was a plank with five men clinging to it, and by kicking my legs and swinging my arms I managed to reach it and clung on. I was seven hours clinging to this piece of wood. One man, who was a good swimmer, calmly swam off towards the destroyer *Highlander* which was picking up survivors.

Thick black fuel oil from the *Lancastria* stained our skins ebony. It was nearly dark, and we had almost given up hope of ever being rescued, when a small boat came towards us and hauled us in. It was one of the lifeboats from the *Lancastria.*

There is a great deal more detail in Joe Sweeney's graphic account, which I will not quote here, as it was not actually part of my own experience.

I recently spoke to a lady who was a nurse in the City Hospital, Plymouth. She was one of the nurses who tended the injured men brought in from the *Lancastria.* She said they were all in a terrible state and unfortunately most of them died. They were badly burned and had to be given morphine, and their clothes cut away from them. I mention this as the official version released afterwards, said there was no burning oil, but I personally saw patches of flame on the water.

Another lady who was in the ATS stationed at Devonport, was given the job of sorting through the salvage from the *Lancastria,* and found drawings done by the children of the crew who had been drowned. These drawings had probably been hung up in their fathers' cabins. She said she shed tears as this task was so distressing.

We were completely ignorant of the fact that we were witnessing the most terrible loss of life and the biggest sea disaster ever known for one single ship, the losses were greater than those on the *Titanic* or *Lusitania,* or for any battleship, and yet it has been less well documented.

Mr Churchill would not allow the news to be given out to

the people of this country at that time, so soon after the evacuation of Dunkirk. Later he was to admit that it was the worst sea disaster of either the First or Second World Wars. Strangely enough, even today hardly anyone knows anything about it, except those who had lost relatives or knew someone on board.

The official figures of those lost were put at 4,250 but eye-witnesses and people who were actually on board have said it was many more than that, and could even be as many as 7,000. About 2,000 souls were saved.

Nobody had a full list of those who were on board, but one officer, who had listed over 4,000, believed the total number of people on board the ship was more like 9,000.

News of this disaster eventually came out through American sources some weeks later and then it was reported in one of our Sunday papers.

There is some disagreement among survivors as to whether the oil was burning on the surface of the sea, but from the nurse's account and my own observations, there was some fire on the water.

Suddenly, this country began to realise the might of the German Luftwaffe, which had been built up, like their navy, while England refused to believe this could happen – all except Winston Churchill who saw this situation coming and had warned the British government, only to be called a warmonger. As so often happened, the 'voice crying in the wilderness' was right, while the rest turned a deaf ear.

The last I saw of the *Lancastria* was her stern standing straight up out of the sea, with men still desperately hanging onto it. The scene was etched indelibly in my memory.

Chapter Four

After leaving the side of the *Lancastria* we headed off to find another ship. The French tender we were on was still being strafed and bombs were falling all round us into the water, but the French crew bravely managed to get us over to the liner *Oronsay*, a similar ship to the *Lancastria*, of about 20,000 tons, which was lying about a quarter of a mile away.

We did not know it at the time but the *Oronsay* had already been bombed about three hours earlier, and the bridge had been blown off and all the steering put out of action. Also the engines had been badly damaged. If the captain had not had the foresight to cover the bridge with concrete slabs, no doubt this ship would have been sunk as well.

The crew of the *Oronsay* were out in the lifeboats picking up survivors from the *Lancastria*, and rescued many hundreds of them and brought them on board. The destroyer *Highlander* was also picking up survivors.

I was told later that we had about 7,000 men on board, which I am told was the greatest number ever carried on one ship, in war or peace time.

The engineers of the *Oronsay* worked for hours repairing the engines, and also fixing up the auxiliary manual steering in the stern, as the main steering from the bridge had been blown out. Seven thousand men owed their lives to this captain and crew and we cannot thank them enough.

I turned to the chap next to me and said, 'If it wasn't for those silly delays, which were so frustrating at the time, we should have been on the *Lancastria* and probably drowned by now.'

One of our officers, who was looking very white, turned to me and said, 'We have had a very lucky escape.' Even then we were not at all safe, as the planes were still flying round us dropping bombs.

Very few words were spoken by anyone on that ship, as we were all shocked and stunned by the awful sight we had seen already, and it was still touch and go whether the *Oronsay* would even be able to sail.

We were all standing shoulder to shoulder, filling the decks. Gradually, we made our way down companion-ways to the lower regions of the ship, which I was not very keen about, thinking that if we were bombed we would never get out.

Some men who had come from the front line were in a state of shock, some standing white and trembling, and I saw one man who was actually hysterical.

As dusk began to fall, the *Oronsay* shuddered into life, and we began gradually to move, heading for England. The bombers were now all gone, leaving behind their trail of horror. We proceeded at a very slow speed, due to the damaged engines. Many of the dead had to be buried at sea on the way over.

We huddled together and tried to get a bit of rest, wherever we could sit or lie. I think my mind went absolutely blank as I cannot remember anything about the journey.

After sailing through the night, we eventually arrived off the port of Falmouth, Cornwall, where the injured were taken off by tender and put ashore to be taken to various hospitals in Devon and Cornwall. It was not until a long time afterwards that I found out we had called at Falmouth, so I think I must have slept a long time without knowing it.

We then made our slow way up to Liverpool, and when we arrived we found a small crowd of people who gave us a cheer. I was pleasantly surprised to see a man with a cart load of fish and chips, which he handed out to us and would accept no pay. I think they were the best fish and chips I ever tasted in my life.

We were all handed cards by the WVS so that we could write

home saying we were safe, but as it happened I arrived home before the card.

My parents were surprised to see me, and had no idea I had been in France. They had never heard a word about the *Lancastria*, or St Nazaire, and when I told anybody about my experiences they thought I was exaggerating and would not believe me. It was not reported in the papers until many weeks later, and then the full story was not told, as people were still in shock after Dunkirk. The news was first broken in American papers.

Such terrible things were going on at that dark time in Britain's history, that people did not seem able to take it all in.

This episode ended my first five months in the army, when I had gone from 'the phoney war' in England, to the real hell of war, then back again.

I was given the privilege of forty-eight hours' leave. This was called Survivor's Leave.

In wartime, one very often got separated from friends, as people were sent off in different directions. I had lost touch with my friend Derek, as I had not found him among the crowd on board the *Oronsay*. However, after making enquiries, I heard that he had arrived safely back home in England on a destroyer. That was the last I heard of him, life took us in different directions and we never met up again.

After my experiences in France I no longer felt like a raw recruit, but the army does not allow those feelings to last very long. At least I could hold my head up, and treat the new recruits in the manner in which I was treated!

Mr Churchill in his history of the Second World War reveals how he arbitrarily censored the news of Britain's Greatest Maritime Tragedy. He described the bombing on 17 June 1940 at St Nazaire, of the 20,000 ton liner *Lancastria* with 5,000 men on board (eyewitnesses have said there were eight or nine thousand). When the news came he forbade its publication, saying 'The newspapers have got quite enough disaster for today at least.'

He had intended to release the news a few days later, but

events crowded upon him so thick and so quickly that he forgot to lift the ban, and it was some time before the knowledge of this horror became public.

Although more than 4,000 were proved to have perished, Churchill's ban has lasted until today, because the story never captured the attention of the media.

Nobody ever knew how many embarked on the *Lancastria*. There are still widows and next of kin who do not know how their loved ones died. Many of them are buried in France, and there is now a plaque at St Nazaire to commemmorate this awful tragedy.

So many people still have not even heard of it, and when the *Lancastria* is mentioned they look completely blank.

Chapter Five

My next posting was to Donington Camp, the venue of the famous car-racing track. We spent most of the time on rifle practice – I think I may have hit the target once – lectures on how to run a railway, laying railway lines then taking them up again and route marches which were supposed to toughen us up, and heaven knows I needed that! We thought a lot of it was a waste of time but I suppose they had to keep us busy.

Our captain, on the route marches, was always very smart, with his pack neater and better shaped than anyone else's, and he never seemed to get as tired as we did. We had a suspicion, and I am sure it was right, that he had an empty cardboard box packing it out, whilst our packs were heavy with kit and clothes.

One day, we had a delivery of six new motor cycles direct from the factory, for the use of our despatch riders. I could see the latter were getting quite excited and they wanted to get on them and have a ride round to try them out. As there was no officer about, they mounted them and drove off, and of course went on to the race track, where they had a good old burn-up. I knew that any new machine had to be run in, and I waited around to see what happened when they got back. When they eventually did come back, their engines were smelling and very much overheated, in fact they had done so much damage that the machines had to be returned to the factory for an overhaul.

One evening, we were all invited to a concert in the dining hall, where a stage had been erected. A recital was to be given by the celebrated violinist Ida Handl. I was very keen to attend this, as I played the violin, and was very fond of classical music.

The front row of chairs in front of the stage were taken up by the officers, with the CO and his wife in the middle. Ida Handl came on stage with her pianist and the concert started off very enjoyably but, as she was warming up to a very difficult piece by Paganini, I think the CO's wife was getting bored. She picked up a large bag she had with her and took out her knitting. Ida Handl was bashing away on her violin and the CO's wife was clicking away on her needles, seemingly trying to keep up with the music. She was very near to the artiste, and I thought to myself, something's going to give soon. And it did. Ida Handl stopped playing in the middle of her piece and stalked off the stage followed by her pianist. The CO's wife kept on knitting, and hadn't got a clue of the reason. The pianist then came back on stage and requested the lady in the front row who was knitting to please stop, or the recital would not continue. I bet the CO told his wife where to stuff her knitting when they got home!

When we were at a loose end and the officers wanted a rest, they split us into small groups to do jobs around the camp. On one occasion, another chap and myself, were sent to help clean up in the NAAFI tent. This was more to my liking. We reported to the sergeant who was in charge, who was an Australian in British army uniform (which I never quite understood). He was a big man with a loud mouth and was obviously not one to be crossed. His first words to us were 'I hope you bastards are better than the last lot!'

I said to my colleague, 'Seeing he's a sergeant and twice as big as us, us bastards had better keep quiet and get on with the job!' In later years, when living amongst the Aussies, I realised that the word 'bastard' was more of a form of endearment than anything else.

It seemed that his biggest worry was having his cigarettes stolen. He had carefully arranged them himself, in two piles on the counter and made them into neat pyramids, so that if one packet was taken from the top, he would notice it right away. He didn't realise what he was up against with us 'bastards'.

As we were cleaning up and stacking shelves, we devised a way of getting a few packets of his cigarettes. While he was away, doing some checking up at the back of the tent, I kept watch while my partner, who was a proper rogue, removed three packets from each pyramid and re-arranged the pile so that it looked exactly as before. He never noticed it, but I was relieved that we did not have to go back there next day.

We had very little entertainment in that camp, and the high spot of the day was to walk into the next village and have half a pint of beer and four penn'orth of chips.

One day, we did a five-mile run and, although I came in nearly last, at least I did run all the way. I saw some fellows who passed me on a coal lorry, waving and laughing their sides sore, these came in first. There were always a few who enjoyed cheating.

When I was on guard one day, the orderly officer came round to inspect the guard, which is the usual practice in any camp. The guard turned out and lined up – three were very tall and one was short. As we brought our rifles to the inspection position, one man accidentally fired a shot. Luckily, the man beside him was the short one, and the bullet shot over his head, but if the short man had had the accident, the tall man on his right would have had his head blown off.

I was surprised and disgusted at the waste of food in this camp. For supper we could go along and have a Welsh rarebit or cheese on toast, and the amount supplied was for probably a hundred men, but this was only eaten by about twenty, and the rest was thrown out into a bin as pig-swill. Considering the strict rationing for the civilian population outside, I felt it was a wicked waste.

It was always noticeable that men who had come from poor backgrounds were the ones who did the most complaining and were more wasteful. I even saw the cooks throw sugar on the fire to get it started. I thought of the people outside the army who would have welcomed that sugar.

We were getting worse news every day of the state of the war front, with our ships being sunk and the bombings in the cities, and there was no sign at this time of America coming into the war. This country was really on its own and the threat of an invasion was always imminent. Hitler and his gang seemed to be getting stronger every day and we were getting weaker. Of course, Russia was not in the war either at this time, in fact Hitler had a Peace Agreement with Stalin. Things were really looking black for poor little Britain and we seemed to be able to do so little to help. Even General Montgomery had not been heard of, and Hitler and Mussolini between them had control of about three-quarters of all Europe. People today cannot begin to realise how near we were to being taken over by Germany.

Chapter Six

It was now the summer of 1940 and the war was no longer phoney. During the time I spent at Donington Camp it was beginning to change rapidly.

The French had signed an Armistice with the Germans at Compiègne, where the Germans had been forced to sign in the First World War. Britain now stood alone against the might of the German armed forces, which had now been joined by Mussolini's troops, as he was hoping to gain some spoils of war for his own country.

Hitler was now mobilising his forces for the invasion of England and we had precious little to defend us. The French had refused to destroy their navy, which was at anchor at Oran on the French coast, and a part of the British fleet had to go in and put them out of action, otherwise Hitler would have used them against us. This did cause a lot of bad feeling from the French, as many of their sailors were killed and wounded.

The Battle of Britain had just begun, and our Spitfires and Hurricanes were fighting for their lives over the south coast. Mr Churchill made his never-to-be forgotten speech to the British people, 'In the field of human conflict was so much owed by so many to so few.' So many German bombers were shot down by our brave pilots that the Germans switched to night bombing, which left many of our cities in ruins.

Mussolini was attacking Greece, and some British forces were sent out to fight with the Greeks, having great success on that front. Also our Fleet Air Arm attacked and crippled the Italian Fleet at Taranto and we were also beating the Italians in the African desert.

With all this going on our small unit of the Royal Engineers was ordered abroad once again. We were put on a train and sent to Scotland, where we embarked for Egypt. First, we were put on board the French liner *Pasteur*, which looked to be a very magnificent ship, and I thought to myself this would be like going on a luxury cruise.

To get to our quarters, we passed through a most beautiful dining-room and ballroom, where the officers were sitting around drinking whiskies and gins and looking very pleased with themselves. But when we arrived at our quarters we were in for a real shock – what a contrast! We were led right down into the bowels of the ship where the cooking was done for the lower-class passengers. My hammock was slung right over the large vessels for cooking the soup, and if I had fallen out of my hammock I would probably been dished out to the whole ship's company.

Luckily for us, the *Pasteur* had developed a fault in the engine room and could not sail; we were thankfully transferred to the *Cape Town Castle*, a very fine ship. We were given bunk beds in the lounge. This was a very clean ship in great contrast to the *Pasteur*, which I was told had cockroaches in the kitchen.

Before we were allowed to send off any letters, we had a lecture to tell us what we must not write, such as the name of the ship, date of sailing, how many ships in the convoy, and what was our destination. After having those instructions, the officer who was censoring the letters called us all together and read part of a letter one soldier had written home – he had carefully given all the details of the convoy, also destination, which proved a censor was certainly needed.

After leaving the coast of Scotland, we joined a very large convoy escorted by a battleship and a number of destroyers. We were very glad to get away from Scotland, as it was very cold, and there were icicles hanging on the rigging. I never realised that Scotland could get as cold as that.

Some days after we started, I was knocked out by a severe bout of flu; many had the same complaint but my temperature went so high that I was put in the ship's hospital. I must have been very ill as all I can remember was getting into bed and out again when I had recovered. My mates told me that there had been a terrible storm and everybody was seasick but I knew nothing about it.

Always at the back of my mind was the horrific scene I had witnessed when the *Lancastria* went down. At night sometimes I had nightmares when I would visualise all those bobbing heads and oil-covered bodies, and wondered how many of them could have been saved.

Being on the sea again, I was only too well aware that there was always the risk of an attack by submarine, as in the Atlantic and Channel at this time the convoys were being attacked regularly. The so-called wolf-packs of submarines sank millions of tons of shipping around this time and thousands of lives had been lost.

In after life, having read more about the dangers faced every day by the merchant seamen and the Royal Navy, which they faced with the utmost bravery, I realised the wonderful and selfless tasks they performed, which were never properly recognised. The engineers and those below decks in the ships had no chance whatsoever, yet it did not deter them from doing their duty. Nelson would have been proud of them.

One merchant seaman, who had had his ship blown up from under him twice and had suffered terrible privations, when home on survivor's leave was presented with a white feather by a lady, as he was wearing civvies. Of course she did not understand.

The Germans had a plane called the Condor, which had a very long range, and was used for spotting the convoys, and then transmitting their locations to the submarine commanders.

As we got down to the coast of Africa we felt safer, but we were never in reality out of the reach of the U-boats. Of course, we could not allow ourselves to dwell on these dangers, but got on with the everyday life on the ship.

Our convoy consisted of about twenty vessels of different types and sizes, from liners and cargo ships to destroyers and frigates, the latter weaving to and fro around us like sheepdogs with a flock of sheep. They must have had a very difficult time trying to keep us all together and making sure every ship was in its proper station and chivvying up the stragglers. Sometimes they lost sight of a ship in the trough of the waves, and some slowed up due to engine trouble which then had to be escorted at a slower pace.

The *Monarch of Bermuda* stayed on our port bow through the whole of the journey, looking a magnificent sight. It was a source of great interest to me especially as I had come from the centre of the industrial Midlands and had very little experience of the sea. I think now, on looking back, we were very lucky not to have been attacked by submarines, as it would certainly have been worth their while.

As we moved further south, it became very hot, the weather was perfect and a lot of our men were lying about on the deck sunbathing with their shirts off. They had not reckoned with the ferocity of the sun and sea winds, and this caused them to have severe sunburn. Many had the skin hanging from their backs, but the medical officer had no sympathy for them and they had to put up with the discomfort.

On occasions, I was put on duty in the dining-room, so had my meal at midday with the ship's cooks. I was very pleased about this, as I found that cooks had much better meals than what was given to the troops. The only trouble was that it became rather embarrassing as the chef was always trying to feel our legs. I thought he was a bit simple, being very innocent, but eventually he must have found the right legs as one of the men assisting in the kitchen was given a gold cigarette case by him at the end of the trip. I had a lot to learn in those days but now I know what he was after.

We were strictly rationed with water, and it was only switched on for one hour in the morning and one hour in the evening, so there was always a big rush to get washed and shaved. We were able to have a bath, but it was in salt water and it was difficult to get a lather with the soap we had.

We had regular lifeboat drill, putting on our lifejackets, and I was allocated to be in charge of a small raft that would hold about ten men. When I looked at it, I thought, God help us if anything does happen.

Sometimes we played games on deck, such as deck quoits, and also we had to run round the deck so many times every morning, to try and keep fit. There were also boxing matches and in the evenings we played Housey-housey (Bingo).

My bunk was very near to the entrance of the sergeants' mess and my pal, who had been made up to a sergeant, would bring drinks out for me, as were not able to get them otherwise.

Our first port of call was Gibraltar, to pick up provisions and water. Unfortunately no one was allowed to go ashore. The weather was hot and beautiful, and I could see the great rock shining in the sunlight, it looked like a very interesting place, but we just had to look at it from a distance.

We were berthed inside the harbour alongside an aircraft carrier, and were told it was the Ark Royal, but could not see any name on it of course.

After leaving Gibraltar, we headed straight out into the Atlantic again; I was told by one of the crew that we were probably half-way over towards America in order to dodge the U-boats.

After some more days at sea, our next port of call was Freetown, on the West coast of Africa – it was known then as the 'Fever Coast'. In those days nobody would ever think of going on holiday to such a hot and god-forsaken place. We were not allowed to go on shore for fear of catching a fever, and we were also given lime juice for vitamin C. Nearly everybody slept on deck while we were there, because it was so hot the cabins were like ovens – there was no air-conditioning.

We were much entertained by native boys, who came out in bum-boats. We would throw coins into the sea and they would dive down and collect them. They were able to go down very deep, probably about fifty feet or more. We could tell that troopships had called there before, because their language was absolutely disgusting. They probably did not realise what they were saying, but just repeated what they had heard. The nurses and other females on board must have been very embarrassed in those days.

After a short stop there, we then set off for our next destination, a trip around the Cape. The convoy was then split up, half going into Cape Town and the other half to Durban, our ship went into Cape Town.

This time, we were allowed some shore leave and, when we left the ship, people were lined up on the quay to pick us up and give us a good time. A friend of mine and I were lucky as a doctor and his wife invited us to their beautiful house with a swimming pool. They also took us on a sightseeing tour in their car to see the Table Mountain and General Smuts's residence. After the tour, they took us home, and gave us a high tea of bacon and three eggs, followed by ice-cream and melon. This was a real treat.

The next day a Boer grape farmer took us to his estate, where there were countless rows of grape vines. The black workers were sitting around in their shacks smoking their pipes, looking very contented. When we were walking round, two young girls who were his daughters, started pelting us with grapes, and everybody was laughing.

They took us indoors to their very large farmhouse, and we were taken into the kitchen and sat down at a long wooden table, where we were joined by all the white workers. The meal was served to us by black maids in very smart white aprons. The food consisted of meat balls the size of cricket balls, with vegetables, and we felt extremely full after it. It was marvellous weather, and we were told that they only had about one week of winter. It looked a most beautiful place to live.

After three days' leave, we set sail for Port Tufic via Madagascar, the Indian Ocean, Gulf of Aden and the Red Sea. This was the end of our sea trip, and then we went on by train to Cairo – a very miserable and hot journey. All this time we were wondering where we would eventually finish up, as we were never told anything.

Every station we stopped at had young boys selling eggs and bread. The eggs were very small and looked to me like pigeons' eggs. They were also selling bottles of whisky which were very cheap, but later turned out to contain coloured water. They had a way of drilling a hole in the bottom of the bottle and substituting the whisky with water. I never bought any of it but a few had unpleasant surprises.

At length we were camped out in tents on the sand on the outskirts of Cairo and, although it was very hot during the day, it seemed to go below freezing at night.

I was lucky enough to have a day's leave in Cairo, so another chap called Fred Jones and myself went off into Cairo to see the sights. I said to Jones, 'I would love to see the Pyramids and the Sphinx,' and he agreed eagerly, but when we had sorted our money out, we realised we couldn't afford it, and also we would not have had enough time anyway.

As we were walking through Cairo, we were followed by hordes of ragged urchins begging for cigarettes or money, and wanting to clean our boots.

I think my pal and I must have looked like proper suckers, as presently we were stopped by a well-dressed man, wearing a fez, and invited to go with him on a sightseeing tour of Cairo. He looked like a proper spiv so we told him emphatically that we had very little money, therefore could not take up his offer, but he insisted so much and also called a horse-drawn carriage and almost pushed us into it. We thought that perhaps he was just being kind-hearted, so we went along with him feeling very pleased with ourselves. He took us all round the sights of Cairo, telling us all about them in perfect English, and also insisted on our having our fortunes told in the sand. Neither of us could understand a word of what the old fortune-teller said, but it sounded good.

It was a very enjoyable and interesting tour, but at the end of it the inevitable happened – the spiv demanded money from us, but we told him again that we hardly had any. He got very upset and started waving his arms and getting very excited, so we gave him the few shillings we had in our pockets. He looked very angry, and had to pay the driver of the carriage himself. I did have a 10s. note in my wallet but didn't happen to mention it to him.

Chapter Seven

After about three days we moved off from Cairo in a train bound for Alexandria, and I said to my pal, 'I wonder where the hell we are going next.' He said, 'I don't think anybody knows, I think they are just kicking us around until they lose us.'

We were given three very large hard biscuits which you couldn't break with a hammer, and told that this was probably all we would have to eat for the next three days.

When we arrived in Alexandria we were taken to the docks and put on board the Australian cruiser *Perth* to be taken to Greece. We cheered up considerably when we were given a marvellous meal by the ship's cook so, feeling very replete we felt ready for anything. But a little later, as it was getting dark, we were escorted by a sailor right down into the bowels of the ship and put into a hold, which was a bulkhead compartment. There were about fifty of us altogether and we settled down as best we could on the metal flooring to try to get some sleep. The Aussie sailor wished us goodnight, and told us not to worry if we were torpedoed, as the shell of the ship was very thin and a torpedo would go straight through and not sink us. I think he had a warped sense of humour. He climbed back through the hatch, closed it down and screwed it tight. I don't think anybody slept that night, as it was so claustrophobic but luckily we got to Greece without incident the next morning.

We docked in the port of Piraeus, and noticed that we were being counted off by men in civvies, who turned out to be Germans. The Germans were not at that moment at war with Greece, so we could do nothing about it. They all looked very cocky. It was a queer situation, as we were of course at war with them.

All of us piled into lorries and were taken to a small town called New Phalleron just outside Athens, and quite near the port of Piraeus. I wondered for the hundredth time, What the hell are we doing here and is this our final destination?

When we first arrived in Greece, the weather was very cold and it was snowing, which was very unusual there at this time of year, which was about the middle of February.

Most of the unit was posted along the Greek railway network, to assist in the co-ordination of troop movements and provisions. We took over a large house and set up our headquarters. The officers were given accommodation in the bedrooms, but NCOs and men had to pitch tents outside.

My job there was mostly on the telephone, keeping in touch with the men in forward positions. It was not easy to get information, as there was so much interference on the line, which came from the German so-called spies, listening in to any conversations on the telephone.

We had photographs of these spies pinned on the wall but I was never told what to do if we saw any. It may sound very peculiar, but although I was in HQ I can quite truthfully say I hadn't a clue of what was going on or what I was supposed to do. Many letters went backwards and forwards from various officers but I think this was just to keep themselves busy and look important. One day I had a telephone call from an officer and naturally he did not want to say on the line where he was phoning from as the Germans were listening, so he told me to look at the list I had of all the various places where our people were stationed. He said, 'I won't say the name, but look at your list and you will see where I am, when I say "the place with the inscrutable smile".' The place of course was the Sphinx but I am sure any intelligent German would quite easily deduce that.

I was very keen to visit Athens on my day off and, as the war there had not yet started in earnest, I suggested to my pal Fred that we should go and do a bit of sightseeing. I had read quite a lot about Athens, and was determined to see as much of it as I could, so we set off to walk the four miles into the city.

We found Athens to be a very fine city surrounded by hills, and about four miles from the sea. As we passed through the outskirts, we thought they seemed very run-down and dirty. I had read that it was one of the most ancient cities of the civilised world. The Acropolis, the hill crowned by the Parthenon, outside Athens was a magnificent sight. The day we visited Athens we had perfect weather, which was lucky after the cold and snow.

I was surprised to find that the centre of the city seemed to be quite modern, with many of the buildings built with white marble in the classical style. We had a good long walk around Athens and also took a ride on the underground railway, which was quite a surprise as I did not not know they had one until I saw the entrance to it.

As we strolled around, taking in all the interesting sights, we saw the Greek soldiers, called *evzones* I was told, marching up and down guarding the king's palace. They looked like ballerinas to us and we stood staring at them for quite a time. They were clad in white dresses with short, pleated skirts, caps with long tassels with a bobble on the end, with shoes with upturned toes with black bobbles and long white stockings. I said to Fred, 'I'm glad that we haven't got to wear that gear, we could never keep it clean.'

By this time we were getting quite tired with all the walking and needed a rest. My pal noticed a queue of British soldiers waiting, as he thought, to go into a picture house. He said, 'Come on, let's join the queue, and go in, it'll give us a rest, even if we don't understand the language.'

On seeing the soldiers looking so excited and so eager to get in, we thought it must be a good film. The queue started to move along, and we went through the door with the rest of them. When we got inside, I said to Fred 'This is a funny sort of cinema.' There was a strong smell of cheap scent and lots of doors with fancy curtains on them. In the middle of the hall was a large staircase and, coming slowly down the stairs, was a very beautiful young lady dressed in very flimsy black underwear.

Fred said to me, 'They have better usherettes in here than we do in England.' As we were enjoying this beautiful sight, a lot more not-so-beautiful girls came out of the doors with the fancy curtains. They were dressed (or undressed) in the same way as the one coming down the stairs. I thought to myself, This is a queer set-up. Then one of the girls made a grab for my cap. As quick as lightning I chased her and grabbed it back, yelling to Fred, 'Let's get out of here,' and we got to the door as quickly as we could. When we were safely outside, I said to Fred, 'You bloody idiot, that was a brothel.' I think we were probably the most stupid and innocent soldiers in the British army. I was told later by another soldier, who had taken advantage of their hospitality, that grabbing the cap was a ruse to get you through the door and onto the bed. We also heard that you were likely to get your wallet stolen while enjoying yourself.

It was surprising the numbers of soldiers that visited brothels, considering the lectures and warnings we had from our medical officer as to the dangers this could incur.

Later that day, we went on to visit the Acropolis, which was quite a steep climb. There were very few people about, except for some Greek soldiers who seemed to be checking on any sightseers. We saw the Forum, and then walked over to the Parthenon. I felt a certain amount of awe to think of the age of these places, which had been built long before Christianity had even been heard of.

While we were up there, three German planes flew over fairly low down, looking rather ominous to us. The Germans were not yet at war with Greece but we felt a premonition that their interest in these parts was not entirely friendly.

In the evening we visited a night-club, down in a cellar, where a very young girl was singing accompanied by a string band. The noise was terrible but after a few drinks of their local brew which was called ouzo, it began to sound much better. This drink tasted like aniseed, looked like water and did not appear to be very strong but it made us slightly drunk. Unfortunately, next day, every time we took anything to drink,

Unfortunately, next day, every time we took anything to drink, we became quite drunk again, so it must have been powerful stuff. We stuck to beer after that.

One evening we walked down to the port of Piraeus. There were some small cottages overlooking the port, and as we were passing one of them an elderly lady who was standing in her doorway called to us, in a slight Lancashire accent: 'Would you boys like to come in and have a cup of tea?'

We were very surprised and gratefully accepted. She asked us a lot of questions about England, as she had not been there for many years. She had been married to a Greek, who had died, and she was left there on her own. The room she took us into was very pleasant, with a view right over the port and the sea. Afterwards, I wondered what had happened to her, because the next day the Germans declared war on Greece and, during that night, they bombed the port of Piraeus and blew up an ammunition ship. The huge explosion almost wrecked the town, the ship's propeller landing right in the centre.

I was five miles away but it shook the whole place. I expected that all the cottages around the port had been flattened and I wondered if the poor lady who had befriended us had survived.

The British ship which had been blown up was the *Clan Fraser*, which had been alongside the quay. It had 200 tons of TNT on board. This attack cost the British and the Greeks eleven ships, with a total tonnage of 43,000 tons. This put the port of Piraeus almost out of action and it was put out of bounds to all British soldiers. As I was stationed right on the coast, I saw about twenty cargo ships of various sizes, anchored off the port, unable to come in.

The day the Germans declared war on Greece I noticed that Athens was full of Greek soldiers, and I was told they had been given leave. We wondered if the German Intelligence, in choosing this particular day, knew this, as if they may have found out that so many Greek troops would be there.

We got the intelligence that the German army had joined up with the Italian army under Mussolini, and were breaking through Allied lines into Greece. We had to try and get in touch with all our troops and bring them back into base, as we were told that Greece was being forced to capitulate, and there was no point in the British contingent staying around any longer.

We began burning up all our documents and gathering our belongings together, ready to evacuate. I thought to myself, I have not been in the Army much more than twelve months, and this is my second evacuation. I hoped we would not have to go through another traumatic experience like we had from St Nazaire.

I wondered what our next destination would be but we ordinary soldiers had never heard the name of Crete mentioned.

Chapter Eight

We were told we had to leave the camp at New Phalleron and we had to get our kit together and move off as quickly as possible. We still had no idea where we were going. I noticed that the Greek carpenter whom we had engaged to make up some mess tables for us was still working on them, and I wondered if he would ever get paid. I expect they came in very handy for the Germans.

We had a very different send-off compared to the waving and smiling of the locals when we had arrived. As we marched away they looked very glum and worried and no wonder as their next visitors would be the Germans whom they hated.

We were marched down to the port of Piraeus and put aboard a small and very old Greek steamer called *Elsie*, the sort of vessel which had been used to travel between the islands. It had two holds for merchandise and passenger accommodation amidships. We were told to find a space on deck.

Very soon we heard the sounds of a big panic on the quay. Large limousines were drawing up; they were in such a rush that they were crashing into each other. All these cars were chauffeur-driven and we guessed that these were very important people. We were instructed to go down and help them with their luggage. We noticed that these people were very expensively dressed; the women were covered with jewellery and carried exquisite fur coats. When we began to carry their baggage, it seemed extremely heavy and I remarked to the next soldier, 'They must have gold bars and the Crown Jewels in here.' Actually, this could have been a good guess, as we heard later that some of them were from the Greek royal family, with their maids and servants, who were later put on a seaplane for Egypt.

While all this was going on, there was a good chance of being attacked by German planes, but luckily for us there were German POWs in the holds of the ship and with the German spies being all round, perhaps this was why we were not bombed. I think we were the only ship which was not attacked by the Stukas that day.

The ship's crew were in a great hurry to get going and we were told that we were going to head for Crete. There is no doubt that this ship would not have sailed for Crete except for the fact that they were taking their own people who were desperate to escape. It is usually a fact that the rich and famous people can find a way of getting to safety, whilst the ordinary people have to stay behind and suffer whatever comes.

We set sail in the evening and saw several planes go over but, although we were completely on our own with no sign of any escort, they left us alone.

About mid-morning next day we arrived in Suda Bay, on the island of Crete. Our illustrious passengers disembarked. After I helped one elderly lady down the gangway of the ship and carried her very heavy luggage, she thanked me in perfect English.

Looking across to the land, I could see hills covered with olive groves, with rocky mountainous country in the distance. Once again I wondered what on earth I was going to do here. The lower ranks never knew from step to step in the army. 'Theirs not to reason why . . .'

The next day the fun started, when the Stukas came over, which had several attempts at bombing us, and managed to sink many other ships in the harbour. We had been hoping to sail on to Alexandria, but the Greek crew refused to take us and we were told they had immobilised the engines.

We used to lie down on the deck of the ship taking the odd pot-shot at the Stukas with our rifles, which of course was quite useless. Incidentally, we were the only ship in Suda Bay which was not sunk or damaged whilst we were on board, although the German prisoners had already been taken off.

37

Eventually we left the ship for shore and took up residence in some old semi-derelict buildings on the hillside overlooking Suda Bay, where we had a good view of all that was going on. The bay was being pounded from dawn to dusk and most of the ships were now on the bottom, after burning fiercely. Near where we were camped around Suda Bay there was a small church with a very tall slim round tower, so my officer suggested I should climb to the top and be a lookout for paratroops landing. I certainly did not relish the idea but had to obey orders. Luckily for me before I got near the church a Stuka dived down and blew the top off the tower. For my part I was quite pleased and rejoined the officer in the slit trench and found him at the bottom as usual. Whenever I had to take cover quickly I always seemed to land on top of him.

I now noticed that the battle-cruiser *York* was in the middle of Suda Bay. It had been sunk by Italian torpedo boats which managed to get through the boom which should have protected the bay and had settled on the bottom, but her deck and superstructure was sticking up above water. The crew were still pounding away at the planes with their guns, which seemed to me remarkably brave as they were obviously sitting ducks. I learned later that it was on the 28 May 1941 that they eventually abandoned ship. This fact was not even mentioned in some accounts I have read by well-known authors. I am giving a true eyewitness account.

Our troops, who were deployed to 'defend' Suda Bay against the Stukas, had very little fire power, and had to use hand grenades shot from the barrels of our rifles, which was next to useless, but gave us the illusion of doing something.

I noticed that as the German bombers came over Suda Bay for the daily 'circus', I heard a sort of 'whooshing' sound from a nearby grove of olive trees about a hundred yards away. The bombers were overhead by this time, and we watched from our dugout in amazement as the whooshing noise was followed by several white objects in the sky, which turned out to be parachutes.

'What the blazes is that?' said one of our chaps in disbelief. 'It must be our b— secret weapon.'

It certainly was, as nobody seemed to know anything about it. We watched in disbelief as the small parachutes floated gently down with what appeared to be a bomb hanging underneath them. The planes, on seeing these, turned away, allowing the parachutes and bombs to float to the ground, and then they came in promptly and plastered us with bombs. The pilots must have been laughing their heads off. We never did find out whose brilliant idea this was, it was a real Heath Robinson affair.

I have since read that this wonderful weapon also had piano wires hanging down, presumably to catch the planes. It was also said that it was never fired, but I can assure you I saw it fired on at least two occasions. It would be interesting to know what the Germans thought of this.

The official name of this gun was an 'Aerial Minethrower' and was probably the only one ever made.

One incident I remember clearly was of Messerschmitts trying to shoot down our three Gladiators. These were the only British planes I had seen over Suda Bay. They were so slow and manoeuvrable that I never saw one hit. I think they must have been trying to make their way back to Egypt.

The next day a British cruiser came into Suda Bay to bring ammunition and stores and our unit was taken on board to go back to Egypt, with the exception of two officers, a sergeant, myself (a lance-corporal) and two sappers. Why they left us on Crete – a railway unit – as there were then no decent roads let alone a railway, we never could understand.

The cruiser was so swift coming in and out that our sergeant got left aboard whilst organising the stores but he bravely jumped into the dock fully clothed and swam to the shore. It might have been better if he had stayed aboard but so many ships were being sunk by the Luftwaffe we shall never know. We heard later that six of our destroyers and cruisers had been sunk and many damaged, including the cruiser *Perth* which was damaged, this being the one which had brought us to Greece.

After the capitulation of Greece we knew we were in for a

rough time, as we had already witnessed the might of the German Luftwaffe.

Many Australians and New Zealanders, who had come straight from their home countries, were landed on Crete. They had no chance to find their feet before they were plunged into war. Greek soldiers were also arriving, ready to take part in fighting with us against the Germans.

General Freyberg, leader of the New Zealand forces, was put in charge of the defence of Crete. It was a daunting task, as he had very few troops and no air defence to speak of, whereas the Germans could drop as many as 15,000 paratroops in a day, plus gliders.

The Cretans were also getting ready to fight, with anything they could lay their hands on, such as shot-guns, swords, pitch-forks, in fact anything with sharp points. They were a warlike lot and thank goodness they were on our side and absolutely hated the Germans.

We had received information that Crete was well protected from any sea invasion from the Germans, for we had almost all the Mediterranean Fleet out there: the battleships *Queen Elizabeth, Barham, Warspite* and *Valiant*, together with about fifty destroyers and cruisers. Out of the battleships, the *Queen Elizabeth* was the only one not to suffer damage, as she had been equipped with guns with a higher trajectory and could raise their guns high enough to fire at the Stukas. Unfortunately, many of our ships were being sunk and damaged by the Stukas, which were attacking them in great numbers.

By this time the German parachutists were coming down around Màleme Airport, which was a few miles from us. They had various coloured parachutes, officers had red or pink, other ranks black, medical were yellow, and ammunition was white. We were waiting for them to arrive at Suda Bay, but thank goodness they were concentrating on Màleme Airport. The New Zealand troops soon put paid to them.

Gliders were also trying to land but many of them were shot to pieces and burning before they reached the ground. The bombers and Stukas were becoming more numerous over us, so much so that one of our Bofors guns opened up to try and shoot one down, and no fewer than three Stukas dived down and attacked it. The crew managed to get clear but the gun was blown up.

The Stukas were now going round in circles, which we nicknamed 'the circus', and attacking every ship and everything that was afloat in Suda Bay – I even saw one attacking a floating log. They would aim the plane at the target and scream down. It was a horrible sound: the Stukas had 'screamers' attached to them and the bombs had a whistling device on their fins. The planes would come over at daylight and would be circling over us and bombing until dusk fell, that was from about 5 am until about 10 pm, as this was the middle of May.

Each plane would be able to do about four or five bombing raids in one day, as they had a base now on the island of Rhodes. Dornier bombers, as well as Messerschmitts were also machine-gunning us. They had machine-guns on the front, sides, and rear, and were able to fly very low as they knew they had no opposition. We had heard that all our aircraft had either been shot down or returned to Egypt.

We could not get away from the air attacks, as they were raking the woods and olive groves with machine-gun and cannon fire, so it was getting a bit too hot for us in the place where we were stationed, and we were getting a bit bomb-happy.

Whilst all this was going on, I was sent out on a patrol with our officer, who, I think, had an even worse sense of direction than I had. We went down the middle of a long, narrow road, past burned-out gliders, and every so often a voice came out of the bushes, 'Get under cover, you silly b—s.' I suggested to the officer that we should turn back, as we seemed to be in no-mans-land. He agreed, and as we turned back I felt a queer sensation in my back as if at any minute I would be shot. It was a good thing that we got out of it when we did, as very soon after this there was an attack by the Germans who, we realised afterwards, had been very near to us and probably thought we were not worth a bullet.

When we got back to our post, where we had dug trenches, the officer was told that one man had 'flipped his lid' and deserted, and the officer ordered me to accompany him to try and find him. His orders to me were 'If we find him, I shall order you to shoot him.' Thank heaven we never did find him as I could not have shot one of our own men in any case and then the officer would certainly have shot me. He was hell-bent on shooting somebody.

The information that we were getting over our field telephone was not very encouraging. It seemed as if the Germans were getting the upper hand and were infiltrating everywhere.

Chapter Nine

One very dark night, we were ordered down to the quayside, and told to wait. We thought that perhaps we were to be evacuated, but no such luck. After a time we heard a quiet ring on the telegraph of a ship, and we heard a movement in the water, then, before we realised what was going on, a cruiser came alongside like a ghost ship. We did not see it until it was a matter of a few yards away. There was a slight bump on the quayside and sailors jumped ashore and tied her up. We helped to unload some boxes of ammunition and we noticed a small body of men come off the ship and vanish into the darkness. Some officers then went on board but that was all we could see or knew. It all happened so quickly and efficiently, it was uncanny. It must have been a brilliant piece of seamanship to get that ship into Suda Bay past all the sunken and damaged ships. We could not see the name of the ship, but hoped it was not one of those which was eventually sunk.

Next day, the bombing started all over again, and a small ship containing ammunition, which had already been bombed once, was hit again. This time a fire was started in the hold where the ammunition was stored. There was an effort made to put the fire out, but the ship eventually blew up.

The Australians and New Zealanders were still trying to defend Màleme Airport, and were having a very tough time. Paratroops were still trying to land there and were being shot up, but the Germans were still sending more in; they seemed to have an endless supply. Most of them were Austrian; we understood they were the cream of the German Army and Hitler was very proud of them. We heard afterwards that their commanding officer, General Student, was losing so many men that Hitler was very angry, and later demoted him to a field officer. This particular episode in the war was such a shock to Hitler's pride, that he never allowed paratroops to be used on any front again.

Nearly 4,000 German troops were killed, and over 2,500 wounded on the first day alone (which was 20 May 1941) and every man who survived the Battle of Crete was awarded the Iron Cross. They also lost 350 aircraft, including 150 Junkers transport planes, and Germany was not able to make up enough transport planes for the Stalingrad airlift later on in the war, so to that extent at least the efforts of Allied troops were not entirely wasted.

Things were warming up to such an extent where we were, that we were relieved when our officer had news over the field telephone that we were to move away from Suda Bay immediately. He was told the Germans could not be held any longer and we were to make our way to Sphakia on the other coast. Very soon after starting out, our two officers joined two other officers in a small lorry, and telling us to make our own way as best we could, they vanished into the distance. What we thought and said about this was not repeatable.

When we left Suda Bay, it was covered by a pall of black smoke from sunken and blazing ships. By this time the Germans had managed to capture Màleme Airfield and were bringing in heavy guns and equipment, also motor bikes. More and more planes were attacking and we could hardly hold our heads up to see what was going on. We were getting rather dazed and shellshocked. With air defence non-existent, we were sitting ducks, with the German planes going round in circles looking for anything to hit. They were also raking the woods and olive groves with fire.

Sphakia on the other coast was a long distance away and it was going to be a long and difficult trek over the mountains.

Even now, Sphakia is the most remote part of Crete, with no proper roads, but only mountain tracks. It is a very sparsely populated area, where any inhabitants keep very much to themselves, and still carry knives and guns.

We realised that our position was pretty hopeless now that the Germans had established an air base at Mâleme. They could get around quicker than us, and were using mountain troops who were used to that sort of terrain.

As we were making our way uphill towards the mountain-sides, we passed through some woods. In a small clearing we found a Vickers machine-gun, set up and loaded with a full belt of ammunition. There were also many small arms left lying about and deserted tents with food left on the tables. I did pick up a revolver, but realising it was not much good to me I threw it away later – now a useless weapon against German machine pistols. I found out later that the camp had been left by about 200 Marines, who had managed to get away on a fast mine-layer which had come into Suda Bay at night. I have since heard that nearly all of them lost their lives due to a German mine blowing up the ship when they entered the port of Trieste.

The Germans were now dropping leaflets over us, saying that the Cretans were committing atrocities against them, and if we did not capitulate very quickly, everybody would suffer.

It was an absolutely beautiful day with the sun blazing down, and I thought how sad it was to see such marvellous scenery at a time when we were fighting for our lives. We never imagined at the time that in the future people would be visiting this place on holidays.

In the middle of the day, in scorching sun, we began to climb up the rocky mountainsides, still trying to head in the direction of Sphakia. At intervals, there were German snipers hidden in the trees, and behind rocks, and the chap next to me got a bullet in his arm. As far as I know he got left behind, like many more.

I was joined by two Australians, who told me they were probably the only ones left of their unit. They did not seem to be affected by the heat of the day as much as I was. We were all dodging around trying to keep out of range of the snipers.

Our only route of escape now was upwards and over the mountains, as the Germans were blocking off other escape routes. As we got farther up over the rocky slopes, we were surprised to find that there were many hundreds of men in front of us, a straggling untidy line of mixed Australian, New Zealand and British troops. We realised now that we were probably the last of the stragglers.

As we got out of the trees and more into the open on the bare, dry and rocky hillsides, we left the ground snipers behind, but were then at the mercy of the planes, which bombed and machine-gunned us continually. In the distance we saw the German Stukas bombing a small Cretan village, and a pall of smoke was rising from it. They were so unprotected that it must have been done for the sheer fun of it and I felt I could never forgive them for that. Afterwards, we found out that the Cretans were accused by the Germans of committing atrocities, and this was their way of punishing them.

The two Australians that had joined us had no rifles to carry, as they had dumped them, having run out of ammunition. They said we might as well dump ours as we also had run out; I took the bolt out of my rifle and threw it into some bushes and after about a hundred yards I dumped the rifle. We had to move as quickly as possible as it was a matter of life or death and not having to carry a rifle was a help in such scorching conditions. We were sweating profusely but could not remove our uniform jackets as it would have been awkward to carry them when we needed both arms to negotiate the rocks.

Our boots were getting badly damaged by the jagged rocks and I had blisters coming on my feet but we had to keep going. We knew that Crete was finished as far as we were concerned, but we still had hopes of being evacuated by the Navy if we could only reach the coast.

By this time, we were very thirsty. We saw a waterwheel by a sort of mill in a little valley and went hopefully down towards it. There was a crowd of men around it trying to drink the water, but there was very little left. When I got some, it tasted absolutely putrid but I managed to swallow it.

We started to climb again, and the sun seemed to be getting even hotter. I came across one poor fellow who was nearly mad with thirst and was on his knees crying out for water. As I had been saving just a drop in my water bottle I allowed him to have a drink but he finished it off. I remember thinking that if someone offered me a glass of water or a million pounds, I would take the water. Later, as things got worse, I saw some men who were so desperate for water that they were drinking their own urine.

When at times some of us managed to catch a rest in the shadow of a rock, thoughts of Dunkirk and St Nazaire went through my mind, and I wondered if I would be lucky enough to get through this time. I couldn't imagine what on earth we were doing here, and what good was done by this whole exercise, and whose idea it was in the first place. Later on, I found out it was Mr Churchill's idea to make an air base for us and stop Germany controlling the Mediterranean. It seemed pointless at the time, but then I suppose all war is like that to the lower ranks who know nothing of what was being planned. Only the end results matter, and ordinary men's lives were cheap.

In my worst moments of depression, I wondered if we had come almost half-way round the world just to die on this Cretan mountainside, but it never crossed my mind that Britain could ever be beaten by Germany. For all that, perhaps we were complacent, and we were certainly ignorant, and few were religious, but the feeling was always there that right would prevail and an aggressor, no matter how powerful, would not be allowed to win this war.

Incidentally, Mr Churchill later said that it was a victory, in spite of the losses, because it delayed Germany from attacking Russia for about two months, and thereby made it too late for the German army to beat the Russians before the winter set in, which happened to be the worst winter for fifty years. Hitler's idea was that Russia would easily be beaten before the winter set in, and none of his army had even been supplied with winter clothing.

At night, we managed to find our way along by narrow tracks and pathways, but at dawn we had to leave them again and tackle the rough mountainsides. The range was known as the White Mountains. Many of the men were completely exhausted and were dropping out of the line to catch a rest but most tried to keep going, with the object of reaching Sphakia and a rescue boat in mind. Also, we knew the Germans weren't far behind us. In full daylight, we were still being strafed by planes.

As we got to the top of one mountain, there was always another one in front of us – they seemed endless. At last we caught sight of the sea in the distance. We had now walked about fifty miles over the mountains and we were completely worn out, with our boots cut to ribbons. All this time, we had no food at all, and only a few mouthfuls of water.

We eventually arrived at Sphakia, hungry and thirsty, but still hopeful of getting a ship back to Egypt. We had to try and take cover among the rocks of the hillsides leading down to the small cove, as by this time the Germans had discovered that this was the evacuation point, as a lot of troops had left from there already, and they were concentrating their bombing and machine-gunning over the area round about.

In the very early morning, before dawn broke, we managed to get down to the beach, only to be told by some officers that there would be no more evacuation from there, as our forces on Crete had now capitulated. This was the morning of 1 June 1941 and, after all our efforts, this was a terrible blow. We wondered what would happen to us now, as we had heard stories of Germans shooting prisoners, and other atrocities.

I saw men emptying their pockets and burning all their paper money. We were then told by an officer to pile our arms (I didn't have any) and stand in a large circle. Somebody was told to show a white flag and he hung his undervest on a rifle, which was the only thing available.

I stood next to an Australian soldier, a fine tall and handsome chap, who took off his shirt and there was a tattoo on his chest which read: 'Death Before Dishonour.' He took his revolver and shot himself in the head. This was a great shock to me and made me wonder what was coming to us all. I always found the Australians were very proud and brave men.

We were now standing in a circle, completely defenceless, and the Germans had now seen us. We were hoping that they had seen our white flag and had the message that we had capitulated. This appeared not to be the case, as mortar fire was coming over our heads, and also three Messerschmitts came down and machine-gunned us. Many in the circle were killed and wounded. I was very lucky as I only had a slight graze by a bullet on one hand.

Our officer still insisted that we should not move. He still had his revolver and would have shot us if we had moved but, after we were attacked twice by the planes, the Austrian mountain troops came down and placed large flags with swastikas on alongside us and sent up Verey lights. Thankfully, we watched the planes turn and fly away.

We knew that many men had escaped to the hills to prevent being captured, hoping for and receiving help from the Cretans, but I thought better of it as information had got through that the Germans were taking terrible reprisals against the Cretans if they were ever caught sheltering an Allied soldier. They were shooting twenty or thirty Cretans at a time if they were caught helping or harbouring any of the Allied troops.

Later we heard that the Gestapo was doing a sweep of Crete looking for any escaped prisoners.

We learned afterwards that submarines were bringing in men and stores to assist the Cretans and gather any intelligence, as it was considered possible that Germany would make a big air base of Crete to control the whole Mediterranean.

We did not know it at the time but the Germans were trying to make sea landings. They were taking a terrible pounding from our Navy, which had an aircraft carrier, four battleships, and up to about fifty cruisers and destroyers all watching out for attempted landings. They were patrolling, day and night, the whole coast of Crete. They were subjected to heavy air attacks and the destroyer *Juno* was sunk and went down in two minutes with terrible loss of life. The cruisers *Dido, Orion* and *Ajax* with four destroyers, caught the German troop convoy and managed to sink about a dozen caiques and three steamers, all crowded with German troops. It was estimated that about 4,000 men lost their lives that night in the sea. When our ships were running out of ammunition, about 5,000

German soldiers escaped the fate of their comrades as they scattered to various small islands.

The battle went on at sea, with very heavy losses and very few of our ships getting away without being sunk or damaged. This operation, which went on for several days, made the Germans realise that seaborne landings were not feasible as the losses were so high, and may have influenced Hitler in not attempting to invade Britain by sea.

Chapter Ten

The men who came to capture us were Austrian mountain troops, with some paratroops. They were equipped with small automatic side-arms which looked like toys compared with our rifles. The ammunition was in long magazines which also acted as handles. The spare magazines were hung around their waists on a belt. I thought how well equipped and efficient they were compared with us.

The German infantry, after they had made a sea landing, were carried round in troop-carriers like large open coaches, with caterpillar tracks the same as tanks. We had never seen anything like this before and we were shocked to see the equipment they had compared with ours.

We wondered now what would happen to us, as we of course had no idea what they would do with us or where we would be going.

The first thing they did was to segregate the officers from the men. We were made to keep our hands above our heads and lined up ready to be marched off. We soon found out that we had got to march back over all the mountains again to where we had come from ... There was no question of any drink or any food, as they had none to give us anyway.

On the way back, we saw some terrible sights, and the taste and smell of death was in the air all the way. Under one tree there was a group of about six British soldiers sitting and lying about as if resting or sleeping, but they were all dead.

I was so tired on the march back that I fell over and went to sleep, but was kicked by a German soldier and ordered back into the line. The walk back lasted about two days, as nobody had any strength left, and I had now been without food and with very little water for seven days.

We were marched to the other side of Suda Bay, which the Germans had ringed with barbed wire. I had huge blisters on my feet and all I wanted to do was sit down, but there was no chance of that.

When we arrived at a compound ringed with barbed wire, a rumour went round that the Germans were going to give us a drink of tea but they couldn't get any milk or sugar. In the state we were in we would believe anything.

We had to queue up for a drink of water from a very slow-running tap in the compound and we had nothing else to eat or drink for the next two days. We were so weak that if we stood up quickly we would fall down again.

The Germans found all our stores, and ate the contents, throwing the tins away, and these we were allowed to pick up to use to get the small amount of very thin soup they doled out. They had confiscated all the food they could find from the Cretans also, so the Cretans now were as badly fed as we were. They had also suffered a great deal at the hands of the Germans. We had heard that if a Cretan killed a German, they would take all the men from a village and kill them in retribution.

One day, in the middle of June, an English-speaking German officer came round and told us with a proud smirk that Germany had attacked Russia. He said they would certainly beat the Russians in about ten weeks. I was very glad to hear this news, and thought he was being very optimistic considering what had happened to Napoleon, and I felt a little glimmer of hope at last.

We were given a card to send home to our families already printed, 'I am a Prisoner of War in Germany and in good health.' You could write your name but nothing else. I saw men who had lost an arm or leg, and were almost dying, but they all had to send the same card. I am not sure whether my family ever received the card, but they told me that my name was given out on the radio by Lord Haw-Haw, the Irishman, William Joyce.

While we were in the compound, I was asked by my sergeant if I would like to go with him and about six others and try for an escape but, considering the number of guards round the camp, I thought it would be impossible, as we would probably be shot when trying to leave.

At this time, small bands of working parties were being taken out by the Germans to bury the dead and do other odd jobs, and we thought this could be one way of getting out. Our sergeant, without any German guard, lined us up and marched us to the gate, which was well guarded. He indicated to the Germans that we were going on a working party, and it was a real shock to us when they actually let us go through the gate. We marched down to Suda Bay, passing hundreds of Germans on the way, who completely ignored us. I just couldn't believe it myself.

The sergeant eventually found a house where a fisherman lived with whom he had been friendly some time before. He and his family made us most welcome and gave us a good meal, which was eaten from a large bowl in the middle of the table. We were all given a spoon and told to help ourselves. Never had food tasted so delicious – it was a stew with big lumps of goat meat in it, and very hot and spicy. There were six of us, and about five of their family who were all dark and looking like pirates, but very kind and friendly. They probably gave us all they had. They knew the Germans would be round to confiscate any livestock, even their goats.

We indicated to the head fisherman that we wanted him to take us on his boat to try and get to Egypt, but he would not consider this, which was quite understandable as we would probably have been sunk and killed and, even if we had got to Egypt, he would never have got back home to his family. After this, we marched back to the camp feeling a lot better for the meal, and still nobody noticed that we had no guard with us.

I was on Crete in that compound for about six weeks, which was a very miserable time as typhoid had broken out and many were dying.

The days were very hot and the nights very cold. I managed

to find a discarded tent-bag, which I was able to get inside to sleep in, and this kept me relatively warm at night, until one day when I went to get a drink of water, it was stolen. My sergeant told me that somebody in his tent had died of typhoid so I could come in and take his place, for which I was very grateful. The thought of catching typhoid myself never crossed my mind.

What food we had was mostly very watery soup, with not even a piece of bread to help it down. I did actually boil up grass to eat, trying anything we could think of to fill the emptiness. By this time, quite a lot were dying from typhoid, and our own medical officer got us to line up for an injection. There was about a thousand of us who had this, and as I was nearly at the end and the only needle he had was getting blunt, I felt it go in like a poker.

We were all so badly bitten by lice and so sore with bites all over our bodies that our medical officer got permission for us to go in the sea which was close by. The salt water made our skins sting very much, but it was a tremendous relief afterwards. Then, we used to sit on the beach, turn our clothes inside out, and pop all the lice, but we never seemed to be able to beat them.

One small incident which remains in my mind, was seeing the Germans making holes in tins of peaches which should have been ours, and drinking the juice then throwing away the tins. Unfortunately, we could not get to them. They must have thought that juice was all there was in the tins. Anybody caught stealing in that camp was made to hold a heavy rock over their heads and bend their knees up and down until they collapsed.

It was not many days after they took Crete that I saw the Germans receiving mail from their homes.

I think that 30 May was the last day that a final effort was made to bring out any troops remaining on Crete. It had been estimated that the number of men left at Sphakia did not exceed 3,000, but later information proved that there were probably double that number. Our ships could not carry all the remaining men and this would have to be the last of the evacuation. At 3 am, 4,000 troops were embarked and carried safely to Alexandria. Our unit did not arrive at Sphakia until all the ships had gone. Upwards of 5,000 Allied troops were left somewhere on Crete and General Wavell ordered them to capitulate. We ourselves were rounded up so quickly and continually bombed that we had no chance of getting away anywhere and, in any case, we were too exhausted to even try to escape although some other groups managed it.

Although about 16,500 men were eventually brought back safely to Egypt, our losses were about 13,000 killed, wounded and taken prisoner, plus nearly 2,000 naval casualties. Later estimates state that the German losses were well over 15,000 in killed and wounded, with about 170 troop-carrying aircraft lost or damaged. The battle was a terrible blow to Goering too, as the 7th Airborne Division was his, and over 5,000 of his best men were killed. The Germans never used their paratroops again.

Hitler's plan was to attack Crete with three Mountain Divisions, 16,000 paratroops and 7,000 troops to be taken in by sea. His air power consisted of 280 Stukas, 150 fighters, 180 reconnaissance planes, 100 Junkers, 530 transport planes and 40 gliders, making a total of 1,280 planes. I doubt if we had any more than 20, some of which were grounded and some flew back to Egypt, as they were useless against such overwhelming force.

Mr Churchill made the following observations on the battle of Crete:

16,5000 men were brought back safely to Egypt, these were almost entirely British and Colonial troops. Nearly 1,000 more were helped to escape later by various Commando enterprises.

Our losses were about 13,000, killed, wounded and taken prisoner. To these must be added nearly 2,000 naval casualties.

Since the war more than 4,000 German graves have been counted in the area of Màleme and Suda Bay, and another 1,000 at Retimo and Heraklion. Besides these, there were very large but unknown numbers drowned at sea, and many more Germans died of their wounds in Greece. In all the enemy must have suffered casualties in killed and wounded of well over 15,000. About 170 troop-carrying aircraft were lost or heavily damaged.

The 7th Airborne Division was the only one which Goering had and it was destroyed in the Battle of Crete. Over 5,000 of his bravest men were killed and the Germans never tried this type of warfare again.

The German losses of their highest class fighting men removed a formidable air and parachute weapon from taking any further part in any battle.

Our naval losses included three cruisers and six destroyers. Out of our four battleships, three were badly damaged and so were many other cruisers and destroyers. It could have been much worse as the Germans had over 1,000 bombers and fighters which could do many sorties a day from their base in Rhodes.

The Battle of Crete held up the attack on the Russian Front for about two months and, as Germany had lost all its troop-carrying aircraft, the factories were not able to replace them before the terrible winter set in.

Chapter Eleven

We left Crete after six weeks or so with no regrets. We were all very weak and emaciated by this time and we thought that nothing could get any worse. We were marched down to Suda Bay and put into the hold of a ship, where we were packed in like sardines. We were allowed up on deck to get some fresh air in batches of about ten at a time, and we were well guarded. After about two days' very slow journey, presumably trying to dodge the British Navy, we arrived back in Greece at the port of Salonika. This turned out to be an even worse place than Crete.

We were taken to the Greek army barracks and lined up. First of all, everyone was segregated – the Jews, Southern Irish and a few Chinese who had apparently come off a cargo ship. A German officer, with a guard on each side of him, walked up and down the ranks. He looked very bad-tempered and was obviously looking for trouble. When he came to an Australian soldier, he saw that he was wearing his hat, and ordered him to remove it. The Aussie took no notice of him – an Aussie and his hat never liked to be parted – so the officer then punched him right in the face and nearly knocked him out, and then confiscated his hat.

We found that the food here was very little better than what we had had on Crete, but in the soup we found the odd lump of meat, which we were told was buffalo. Every morning, we were lined up and sent out on working parties. I always tried to get on the end of the queue, because there was a good chance of them not finding any work for the last stragglers, but, unfortunately, one morning, they started picking men from the back end. You couldn't beat that lot.

The Germans took us to a building on the other side of the town, and at gunpoint made us carry and stack bombs. We knew this was against the Geneva Convention but they would have shot us immediately had we refused.

It is amazing how long the human body can go on in the state we were in, with hardly any food, and suffering from dysentery as many of us were.

One day as we were marched through the town of Salonika on a working party, a Greek girl with a trolley of sweets she was selling, pushed it in amongst us so that we could take some, but a guard saw her and tipped the trolley over into the road and made the poor girl join our ranks. I don't know what happened to her but I hoped they let her go.

The German troops in Salonika were different altogether from the Austrians, who were fairly humane. I think our new captors were Prussians. They were an evil lot, and used to throw bread from a sentry box to the prisoners, then take photographs of the captured troops scrambling for it. I never joined in although I was very, very hungry.

The lavatories were in a block in the middle of the parade ground, just open trenches with boards over them in the open air. One night when they were occupied by a lot of men with dysentery, the Germans in the sentry box machine-gunned them and killed many men. I saw a soldier jump at the barbed wire, I think he had lost his reason as there was no possible chance of getting through, and he was immediately shot. His body was left there on the barbed wire to deter others.

After staying in Salonika for a few weeks, we were marched off to the station and packed into cattle trucks. We were all given a small tin of meat of dubious origin, this was to last us for about three days. Conditions in the truck were horrific, as we were not allowed out for natural functions through the whole of the journey. We were told that some men in a previous trainload, had attempted to escape, so they kept us locked up. Nearly everybody in the truck had dysentery, which made things worse. We did not have anything to drink for three days and were getting dehydrated and it was very hot with not much air, but I managed to get by a small window opening.

Our first stop was in Yugoslavia. A ladies' voluntary organisation had made big vats of soup and they handed it out to us at the station, for which we were most grateful. As long as the Germans didn't have to feed us themselves, they seemed quite happy to let us have it.

At length we arrived in Wolfsberg, in Austria, and entered a large POW camp which was number Stalag 18A. We were issued with metal tags with our numbers on, to hang round our necks as identity numbers. My number was 5012. This was a large camp with three separate compounds, French, British and Russian, each one would probably take about 1,000 men.

The first thing we had to do, was to be deloused, as we were covered in lice, and this was a great relief to us. We had to remove all our clothes and put them in a bundle, tied up with our metal tag, and then had to go into a big shower. I can't remember any soap being issued, but we did get a piece of towel as big as a handkerchief to dry ourselves on, but before we could get dry, our name was called and we had to rush and get our clothes, even if we were still wet, then put them on and line up, with the Germans shouting and screaming at us all the time.

We were all starving when we got there; the French would exchange a piece of bread for any jewellery and watches that we had. We thought this was rather mean, and it must have been reported to the Germans, for they made the French put everything they had acquired on a large table for us to pick up our belongings as we walked through their compound. The French were looking very sheepish about this. I recovered my cheap wristwatch. The Germans were absolute swine, but I always found them completely honest.

The food we were then given was a ladle full of *real* potatoes with a lot of skin. This was the best meal we had had since before being captured.

I remained in this Stalag for about two months. I often walked round looking for my pals from my unit, but I never found any. By now my boots and uniform were getting in a very bad state, and I wondered what they would supply us with. I did get a pair of French army uniform trousers supplied, every pair was the same size and 'fit' everybody. A tall person would look fairly smart but a short person would be very baggy at the knees and have to tuck them inside puttees. We didn't get any boots, and my soles were already right through. We were eventually supplied with British army uniform by the Red Cross, but this was not for many months.

One day, we were full of excitement, as we saw that Red Cross parcels had arrived, but they were stacked in a compound some distance from us. Every day we stood looking at this pile of parcels, wondering when they would be given out. After about a fortnight the Germans decided to distribute them. I was by this time so weak I could hardly stand up straight, as others were also, so we had been looking forward to them eagerly. When they did eventually let us have them, people went mad, and some ate everything the first day. I saw one Australian mixing everything together, cocoa, meat, Carnation milk, etc, and spooning it up with great gusto. I tried to eke mine out a little, being careful not to eat too much at once, as I was afraid of being ill.

The Russians, in their part of the Stalag, were dying like flies from hunger – they never saw any parcels, poor souls. The French were doing well, because they had parcels from home and they were very well fed, having better German rations than we had. The Red Cross parcels really saved our lives, and I am eternally grateful to the Red Cross.

After a short time the Germans were beginning to organise working parties, and on parade one day I was picked out to go on one, with twenty other men. It seemed a good thing to get out of the Stalag, which was such a miserable place, so we almost looked forward to the change.

Chapter Twelve

We had no idea where we were going, it could be a long journey or a short one. As I was still suffering from dysentery, I was worried about travelling, as we would probably be put in a box van on the train and there would be no toilet facilities. The British medical officer had now set up a sick bay in the camp and I was lucky to find one of our medical orderlies. I told him my trouble and he slipped into my hand a packet of opium tablets. I think they were German and he told me to take one every four hours. These worked like a charm and enabled me to travel without any trouble but, when the effects wore off, I was back to square one.

Early next morning we reported to the gate of Stalag 18A and we were issued with a small round loaf of bread, which had to be divided between six men. This bread was made from potato flour, was hard on the outside but very soggy on the inside and there was no taste in it. There was also a very small square of pure white so-called margarine, which was also tasteless. We were told it was made from coal, and this had to be shared between us. We had saved up a bit from our parcels, which was a great help.

We tried to question the guard as to our destination but, as usual, he would not reply and just shook his head. We managed to get a drink of water when we stopped at a station. The only eating or drinking utensil we had was an empty cocoa tin from our Red Cross parcel. When we arrived at the station we were put into a box van, which had partially open sides with bars, so we had a good view of the countryside. It was magnificent scenery – there were mountains all round towering into the sky. The journey took all day, probably because of detours around the mountains, and our van had to be switched to other trains.

We eventually arrived at a town called Villach, which is in Carinthia, Lower Austria, on the river Drau. This was a fine clean-looking place, with wide tree-lined streets and prosperous-looking shops and houses. As we were marched down the main street we noticed the buildings were hung with long red and black Nazi banners with the sinister-looking swastika in the middle. There were loudspeakers in the trees blaring forth martial music as we passed through. There were very fine views of the snow-capped Alps in the distance which marked the border of Austria and Italy.

Quite a lot of people stopped and stared at us as we were being marched through the streets, they probably did not know we were British as we were dressed in such a rag-bag of miscellaneous clothing. We must have looked a pretty pathetic sight, as we were marching to our billet. I was dressed in half British and half French army uniform, with wooden clogs on my feet as my boots had fallen to pieces, with a French army forage cap which came right down over my ears. People in this town looked very prosperous and probably scarcely knew there was a war on. We passed the Grand Hotel, and saw the cigar-smoking German officers going in and out. I thought to myself, When we win the war, and I have made some money, I will go and stay there. But I have never managed it.

Many of the inhabitants were dressed in their beautiful national costumes and everybody looked well dressed and happy, except for some poor Jews we saw walking round looking very sad and worried. They were being forced to wear the yellow Star of David on their long black coats. I wondered if anything happened to them, as we did hear shooting one night a little while after. They were probably all being rounded up to be taken away, as we did not see them again.

One thing which annoyed me considerably, was when some Germans marched past us, singing, *Roll Out the Barrel.*

We arrived at our accommodation to find it was a dirty old cellar underneath an old guest house in one of the back

62

streets, but even this was much better than our previous living quarters. There was very little space to move round in and also the odd rat running round which we tried to kill by throwing our clogs at it.

The men with me at this place were a motley lot with a few regular soldiers who seemed to be able to cope with life better than we conscripts. We had some Aussies and New Zealanders and these also were a tough bunch. Some, like myself, who had had a soft life, found it very hard going, but we had to grin and bear it.

One English conscript was in a bad way with an injured leg and had to be sent back to the Stalag after a few weeks, as gangrene had set in. As soon as anyone was ill, or was unable to work, he was soon got rid of.

One man in the billet, a Scotsman, was a real menace as he was a kleptomaniac. He was small and short but tough and came from the Gorbals in Glasgow. He stole something from everybody in the billet. I only had about three cigarettes and he even stole those. At the time we did not know who was the culprit, but luckily he was sent back to the Stalag and then things stopped disappearing. A long time later, I saw him again in Stalag 18A and he was covered in bruises and had a black eye. I heard that he was still up to his old tricks but when he had stolen from a man from his home town who was bigger and tougher than he was, he was given a good hiding. The padre in the Stalag had tried hard to cure him of his bad ways but had had no luck – he just couldn't help himself as he had been thieving all his life.

When we were out working, we tried to understand a few words of German other than the swear words that the guards shouted at us. One word we got mixed up with was *schnell* – we thought this meant 'slow' as it sounded like 'snail' to us, but we soon found out that it meant 'go quicker'. This caused a bit of confusion for a time. I have since tried to look up in a German-English Dictionary some of the words the guards shouted at us, but have never been able to find them. They may have been Austrian colloquialisms but more likely were some choice swear words.

After a few weeks working, we received our 'pay'. This was not real money but a small piece of paper with the appropriate number of pfennigs printed on it. We were given this 'pay' as we understood that otherwise, according to the Geneva Convention, we should be classed as 'slaves'. We had to give this to the guard and he would do our purchases for us. My first purchase was a toothbrush and then, after working for a few more weeks, I was able to buy a safety razor and blade. It was a real treat to be able to clean my teeth and have a shave.

We were given a midday meal in an old people's home in the centre of the town; the lady in charge gave us as much as she was able, considering the rations she was allowed. Our main meal generally consisted of thin soup, potato balls containing specks of horsemeat, some sauerkraut and a piece of black soggy bread made from potato flour. This of course gave us a lot of flatulence, causing us to be continually breaking wind, in fact at night this was our only entertainment, as it sounded like Beethoven's Fifth Symphony when we all joined in. I remember one man attempted to play 'God Save the King' but he had a nasty accident before he could finish.

Marching to work in the mornings was also a windy time and the guard bringing up the rear in our slipstream got the full blast. He would complain loudly, holding his nose and getting very annoyed. I don't think anybody could translate what he was saying. We told him he should see we got better food.

One day we saw a pamphlet lying about in the old people's home and were able to understand enough to know it was about euthanasia. We had already noticed that old people who were losing their minds were never seen again and a notice of their death was put up on the front door.

There was an English church in Villach; this was the only one to have its bells removed, presumably to make armaments.

After we had been in our wretched billet for about six weeks, we had a visit from a German officer who came round to do an inspection. He spoke to us quite kindly and we asked him if we could have better accommodation. He agreed it was not suitable and ordered that we should be moved elsewhere. He must have been a more humane officer than most, as he sent us a small barrel of beer.

Eventually we were moved out to another guest house outside the town, and put in a much larger room. The only drawback was that all our ablutions and clothes washing was at a pump outside in the back yard and, as winter was coming on, it was exceedingly cold. At five o'clock in the morning on a cold day nobody wanted to do much washing.

Fortunately, before winter really set in, we were moved again to a more suitable building and, as we were to experience the coldest winter for fifty years, we were very glad of the move. This new billet was a wooden building where bars had been put on the windows, with a barbed wire fence all the way round.

Our first job was working in a quarry breaking up rocks with sledgehammers to go into a machine for road making. I had seen prisoners on the cinema screen doing this sort of work, in places like Alcatraz, but I never thought I would be doing the same thing. We were working for the local council, and had to report to the yard at 6 am every morning except Sunday.

I was very fortunate to be picked out, with another chap, to go road sweeping. We had our brushes and shovels and a little hand cart and this was a very pleasant and much sought-after job. As we swept our way around the streets of Villach, we noticed practically every woman, except the oldest, was pregnant – this was probably on the orders of Hitler, to make new little Aryans.

On a day in the summer when we were out road-sweeping, as we meandered in an aimless way down the main street of Villach, pushing a heap of dust from place to place (some of it occasionally found its way into our cart), we noticed a couple of Italian officers passing by. They were strutting like two prize cockerels, their hats covered with waving feathers and were chatting animatedly and probably feeling very important, when two German soldiers approached in the opposite direction and had to pass them. They pretended not to see them, and didn't salute as they should have done, but averted their eyes contemptuously. We noticed with interest that as soon as they had gone past them, the Germans both turned round and spat in a very rude manner. I did notice that the Germans had no respect whatsoever for the Italians and in fact had more for us.

On occasions, after doing a full day's work from 6 am to 6 pm, and very tired, we could be called out to unload a railway wagon, mostly of coal or cement. These wagons were in short supply, and they wanted them for the next day. We did complain a lot, but it made no difference.

One day, a truck of cement arrived at the station to be unloaded in the evening and I was one of the gang picked for the work. I was still pretty weak after the dysentery and, never having done any manual work in my life, it was as much as I could do to pick up a bag of cement. One man in the gang was a bit of a show-off, and made fun of me, showing how he could pick up two bags at once. The New Zealander, who was a Maori called Tommy Rooker, was always friendly towards me. He came over and picked the other chap up complete with his two bags, and threw him into the truck we were loading and then assisted me in my share of the work. I found the Aussies and New Zealanders made good friends and were always ready to help anybody.

One midday when we were being marched through the town to get our meal, the loudspeakers in the trees gave a very loud fanfare, and Hitler started to give a speech. As his voice got louder and louder and more excitable, we just could not contain ourselves and we all joined in, shouting and giving the Nazi salute. The civilians in the street did not seem to be taking much notice of Hitler, but when we joined in I could see some turning their heads away trying to stop themselves from laughing. No German or Austrian would have dared to do what we did and our two guards clicked the safety catches on their rifles and threatened to shoot us. We were not allowed to have our midday meal that day, but it was worth it.

One man we always waved and smiled at when we saw him was the local undertaker. I think he was a bit simple. He was always dressed in his tall black hat with long streamers attached and a long-tailed black coat. We always wished him a 'good and prosperous business'. He always waved back and grinned but probably did not know what we said.

After finishing work and on our way to the old people's home for our midday meal, we were about to cross the road, when at the same time a large military parade, complete with mace-bearer and band, began to block our way. The guard, who was at the back of us, ordered us to halt, but as we were so hungry and looking forward to our meal, we were desperate to get across in front of this lot.

The mace-bearer was already passing us, so I said to the chap next to me, 'Look, we've got to get across quickly or we'll have to wait a long time for our dinner.' It looked like a very long parade, so we rushed across the road, but unfortunately we got between the mace-bearer and the band. He got out of step and nearly dropped his mace, and the band bunched up, losing their formation and their places in the music. This caused absolute chaos, as there were also cars behind containing high- ranking officers, followed by goose-stepping troops. They were all running into each other, and the high-ranking officers were all standing up in the cars and yelling, threatening us with gaol. They also played hell with the guard, who got the worst of it, he nearly got shot. As he was behind us, there wasn't a thing he could have done about it. It had passed through my head that I didn't fancy standing beside the road dressed like the rag-bags we were, while that smartly turned out lot pranced in front of us. We expected to have some sort of punishment for our misbehaviour but I think the officer in charge must have had a sense of humour, as we heard no more about it. We were even allowed to have our dinner.

I think the guard was afraid to tell the camp commandant about the incident in case he was threatened with the Russian Front, which was always something to be dreaded.

After we got back to camp in the evening, we felt we had been very lucky to get away with that escapade, as it was a stupid thing to do, but the funny side of it struck us.

Some time later after we had arrived at the old people's home for our meal and were just about to sit down and begin it, the commandant walked into he room with a lady by his side. He ordered us all to line up and the lady pointed to myself and another POW. I thought we were being picked out for some special job but it turned out we were pointed out to go to gaol. I hadn't the faintest idea what was going on but, as the two of us were being marched out, another man stepped forward and said he was the culprit they wanted and not me, and he took my place. Afterwards, it turned out that the two men had been working in the cellar of the Grand Hotel in Villach, and thinking they were not observed, had peed into a barrel of sauerkraut (pickled cabbage). I don't know what the fuss was about, as it could only have enhanced the flavour. We didn't see these two men for another seven days.

Very often in the wintertime when the snow was very deep, we would be taken off to clear the snow from the narrow side-roads where the snow had drifted up to ten feet or more. People were often trapped in their houses and we would be taken to help dig them out. We were supplied with large shovels, the blades of which had been dipped in hot tar, and this would make the snow shoot off the shovel and made it much easier for working. No snow-ploughs were available in wartime so we were used instead.

Around Christmastime, part of our work was to cut down Christmas trees. This was a miserable job, as they were not very tall, and we would get covered with snow and wet through whilst moving among their branches. Our overcoats would get wet and, by the time we got back to the billet, they would be frozen. In spite of this discomfort and the bad food, we did not have much illness in the camp, it was probably too cold for the germs to survive.

There was a motley lot in this camp too from various walks of life. One chap in the camp told us he was a lord and I believed him as he was a good-looking aristocratic type. Although he had been an officer in the army, he had taken off his pips before being captured so that he could get to a working camp with the idea of escaping. He told us many interesting stories of his escapades with court debutantes, which made our hair curl. These girls must have had nothing better to do than dress up and go to bed with as many men

68

as possible. I don't think he was boasting when he told us how he would move from room to room in some stately home, enjoying himself at night with so many sexy females. He never told us where his home was, or what was his title, but he knew all the best houses in London and had dined at all the best hotels. He told us he had been educated at Eton and was so well-spoken that we all believed him. Of course, it may have been a 'con', but if so it was a very good one. We were glad of any stories to liven up our restricted lives.

Chapter Thirteen

Winter was coming on by this time and it turned out to be the worst in fifty years. The roads were covered in snow and ice, hard pressed to two feet thick and with deep ruts made by the traffic. We were made to chip out the ruts to level the road with pickaxes. This was a rotten job as our clogs got covered in ice which stuck to them and made them very heavy; we had no socks, only folded rags, so our feet were very uncomfortable. It was a great relief that very soon after this we were supplied with British army uniforms and boots from the Red Cross, through Switzerland. All the trousers in the uniforms we were issued with turned out to be size 16s, the largest size in the British army. It took a lot of ingenuity to make them fit, but they were nice and warm. I stitched a large pleat at the back of my trousers and this made the pockets all hang round the back. We also got some socks, which was a great blessing, as the rags would bunch up and make one's feet very sore.

While we were working on the roads one very cold day, an old lady who looked sorry for us came over and threw me a woolly hat when the guard was not looking, and I gratefully put it on – it probably saved my ears from frostbite. I feel eternally grateful to her.

When chipping the ice to level the road in the streets of Villach and we needed to go to the toilet a civilian worker was sent with us as guard. He was an elderly man and also suffered from the extreme cold. He would take us one or two at a time to a local hotel and then we would go down to the boiler room for a quick warm up. It was more for his benefit than ours I think.

I did get frostbite in my fingers and also caught the flu, so was allowed to work in the kitchen taking the skins off hot boiled potatoes, which helped the circulation.

After getting the army boots, the clogs were left in the billet, so we thought the best thing to do with them was to put them on the fire to get a bit of extra warmth. We were angrily told off for doing this but it was too late after they were burned.

Then suddenly it was Christmas. We wanted to celebrate it in some way, so we decided to have a little concert.

On Christmas Day 1941 we were given the day off work, so we decided to have a celebration dinner. We had saved up our tins of spam and this was our 'turkey', and for pudding we had tins of rice pudding and Carnation milk and some biscuits and cheese, together with a little chocolate, all of which came from our Red Cross parcels.

We put the two long pine tables together, and covered them with a tablecloth. This was borrowed from a Polish lady who lived with her family nearby. This family had lived in the hamlet a long time and were accepted as Austrians by the locals. She also did a little mending for us in exchange for a few items from our parcels. When we had laid the table out with borrowed cutlery and cigarettes standing up in little tins, and strewn with greenery, the commandant was so impressed that he brought all the locals in to show how well we were looked after – this was a bit of propaganda, as we had supplied all our own eatables from the Red Cross. Most of the ordinary local people were extremely nice and we never felt any animosity towards them.

In the evening we held a concert, with the tables as a stage. The commandant, who had his wife and daughters staying with him as he was probably unable to get leave, brought his family with him and sat in the front row of chairs. This commandant was a decent, jolly old chap. The 'turns' consisted of one man singing 'Danny Boy' in a good Irish tenor voice, another chap told jokes, which we were glad the audience did not understand, another did a monologue, another who had worked in a circus, did handstands and aerial somersaults, and then came the grand finale. We had made the circus chap a short baby's dress and bonnet with a pair of bloomers, the materials begged from one of the civvies we worked with. He came on to do his act of singing a very sad song, and ended up pretending to cry. When he finished his song, he lifted up his short dress to wipe his eyes, but unfortunately he had forgotten to put on his bloomers. He had nothing on underneath and the commandant's wife and daughters screamed and hid their faces but the commandant laughed his sides sore. They told us afterwards that they had enjoyed the concert very much – I think they were glad of a bit of entertainment the same as we were.

It was then January 1942, and getting very cold indeed. We had to leave the taps running all night or they would have frozen up. It was hard to keep warm with only one tiny stove and the condensation from our breath made the walls run with water. Our bedding consisted of two thin blankets and our overcoats, the latter being nearly always wet through from the day before. When at six o'clock in the morning we opened the door to go off to work a cold white mist would float in. A lot of the men had grown beards, and it was comical to see the icicles hanging down off them before they went very far. In the bitter wind we had to keep batting our eyelids as we were afraid they would freeze up.

When we reported to the council yard for work, we always looked at the large barometer hanging outside to see if it was minus 30 degrees Centigrade or below, as we would be excused work if it was. As it was hung in a sheltered place out of the wind it only reached minus 29 but when working out in the wind or blizzard I am sure it went well below minus 30.

We were suffering in the awful cold weather but at least we knew the Germans were having it even colder on the Russian Front. This exceptionally bad winter had a good effect on the war from the Allies' point of view, as Hitler had expected to beat the Russians before winter set in. We ourselves, of course, knew nothing of their losses in Russia at that time.

We were marched off one very cold but sunny day to a ski slope, just outside Villach. We thought the Germans had had a change of heart towards us and we were going to do some ski-ing. Some hopes! We soon found out when we got there this was not the case. The loose snow at the bottom of the ski slope was not suitable for the skiers to land on, so they arranged us into a line and made us march backwards and forwards stamping down the snow until it was hard enough. At least it kept our feet warm, and really was quite a good job, considering we were POWs. Only one guard was with us, so four of our party slipped away and picked up a large sledge. Our guard was busy looking after us and did not notice them leave. Half-way up the slope, they jumped on the sledge and down the slope they went. The sledge flew away from under them and all four shot down the slope and finished up very badly bruised. Luckily the sledge was not broken, but the guard was very angry and had no sympathy for their discomfort. We were then taken back to the camp and did not get a chance to see any ski-jumping. The four men were reported to the camp commandant, who as usual, threatened us all with the SS – this did not worry us unduly as we had heard it so often before.

One of the more pleasant jobs we had was the delivery of coal to a hotel which was above Lake Faakersee. This was a very small lake but very beautiful and the hotel was on the mountainside overlooking the lake. We had to take the coal out on a horse-drawn cart then load it bag by bag onto the mountain lift, and we would go up on the lift with it to the hotel and unload it into their cellars. It was a beautiful location, and we were told that our Prince of Wales (Duke of Windsor) had stayed there on holiday. The owners never ever spoke to us and never even gave us a cup of coffee.

A little later on, as I had been ill with flu, I was sent back with three others to Stalag 18A again. I was sorry in a way, as I heard there were many worse camps than Villach, but of course I had no choice but to go.

Chapter Fourteen

On arriving back at Stalag 18A I was told there had been an epidemic of typhoid and many men had died. It had started in the Russian compound and had spread to the British and French compounds. The guards did not enter the camp at that time, but left the food at the gate to be collected. Thank goodness it was over by the time I got there.

I had to stay in the Stalag for a few months, which was wintertime again. The Russians were suffering very badly and although I did not witness it myself, I was told that it was not unusual for two Russians to leave a dead comrade outside to freeze up, and then carry his body between them to get his ration. It did not take the Germans very long to realise what was going on and they stopped it.

One very good gadget which was invented by a mechanically minded Aussie in the camp, was called a 'blower'. It was made out of cocoa tins, with a fan in one tin and a handle to turn it, which blew wind into another tin holding small pieces of coal which would glow like a small furnace, and this would boil up your potatoes and warm up the meat from your Red Cross parcel. It created a lot of heat with the small amount of coal we were allocated. It must have looked very comical to see everyone frenziedly turning their little handles on the blowers to get heat up.

One clever chap made a suitcase out of cocoa tins which were flattened out and somehow bent into one another, I never found out how he did it.

When we were called out on parade for the usual roll-call, the camp commandant told us that the British had committed an atrocity against German POWs in England by putting them in handcuffs, and reprisals were to be made. A number of men were picked out and handcuffs were produced. The guard proceeded to handcuff the selected men. We were then all dismissed and returned to our quarters. No sooner were the guards out of sight than a clever individual soon found a way of undoing the handcuffs. A lookout was kept for the return of the guards, which was about four hours later, when the handcuffs were put on again and all looked as before. This happened for a few days, when apparently honour was satisfied on the German side.

I learned shortly that some men had dug a hole below one of the latrines and built a small room which could hold one person. The reason for doing this was that when a POW was attempting to escape, a volunteer would go down into this small room a few days before the escape was to take place, and when roll-call occurred, one man would be missing and the Germans would presume he had escaped. An alert would be called and police and guards in the area would be notified. After a few days when things had quietened down, then the real escape would be attempted. I think quite a few escaped in this way. It was not easy, though, as the perimeter wire was continually patrolled by guards with dogs. It was a bit easier to escape from the working camps, but some men, especially those who had escaped and been captured, were not allowed out from the Stalag for work.

A concert was arranged in the Stalag, and everyone who could perform in any way was rounded up to do a turn. The New Zealand Maoris decided to put on their war dance. There were about thirty of them in this camp and they painted their faces and had grass skirts (goodness knows where they came from) and made spears out of broom handles. They came on the stage with loud shouts and cries, doing their warlike dance with fierce facial expressions and tongues fully out and really looked a fearsome sight. The Germans sitting in the front row looked really scared, they had never seen anything like it before.

We also had some singing with a choir, one man told a few

jokes which we had all heard before, which I hoped the Germans did not understand.

It wasn't long now before I was pushed off to another working camp, this time in Steiermark.

This next was a working camp again. It was a bit larger than most and held about sixty men. I was sent to join a party helping to build a factory, where we did all the labouring and civilians did the actual building. What this place was for we had no idea.

I made a very poor start as we had a visit from some officers from the local barracks, I think they had come to gloat over the POWs. I was busy (!) shovelling sand from a lorry, when they came round to me they stood laughing and one said, 'My five-year-old son could work better than this one.' But little did they know I took it as a compliment.

I was now put in a billet with six others, and two were Australians. One night they pulled the bars off a window and escaped; they were big strong men and I think they had been gradually weakening the bars for some time. As I was a newcomer, the guards seemed to think I had assisted them but no reprisals were taken against me, and nothing more was heard about the Australians and I hoped they had got away.

There was a small band in the camp and one chap who was a professional musician back home played the violin very well. He could also write music and as I played the violin a little I was allowed to join in on occasions. All the men in that camp had clubbed together with their pay for a very long time to buy a violin, a mandolin and a flute. The musician wrote many good tunes, and one which always sticks in my memory (but I am not sure if he did write this) was a song which began, 'Broadway baby lashed to the mast,/ she has no future, but oh! what a past,/ She is the toast of Washington Square!' I can't remember any more of it.

I had one lucky break in this camp, when on the building site the last roof truss was erected on the top of the factory, and the custom in Austria was to place a small fir tree at the highest point of the building. When this was done, everybody working on the building is given a special meal to commemorate the occasion. We of course did not get as good a meal as the civilians, but ours consisted of a small pork chop with potatoes and beetroot, and very enjoyable it was too. This was the first taste of real meat for me since being taken prisoner.

I did not stay very long at this camp, as I was not very popular with the building overseer. He reported me to the camp commandant for poor and slow work, which did not surprise me in the least. The overseer was a very smartly dressed civilian, with a number of large feathers in his Austrian hat and always wore the traditional green loden suit. Apparently, the more feathers an Austrian has in his hat, the more important he is, so he must have been very important. He had a goatee beard and similar features to a goat. I don't know why, but this annoyed me, and one day, feeling very wicked, I made a goat 'maa . . . aa' after he had passed by. This was the last straw for him and he would not allow me on the job again. I was then returned back to the camp and was given the job of carting stones to lay a path and not allowed out.

There was a 'camp representative' in all camps who was chosen by all the men to be a go-between between them and the camp commandant. He was usually the one who could speak the best German. I did not care for this chap, as he seemed to be very much in the pocket of the Germans. He suggested to the camp commandant that I should report sick as they both wanted to get rid of me. I told him I would be delighted to get away, as in my opinion they were all working too hard for the Germans. As it happened, I did not have to go sick and I was returned to Stalag 18A with two others by the end of the week.

Now my health had improved due to the Red Cross parcels, I quite enjoyed a bit of travelling around and seeing different parts of Austria, looking at the beautiful scenery; it was much better than working all the time.

When there were only three or four of us travelling, we were put into a railway compartment to ourselves, which was very comfortable as the rest of the trains were usually quite full. There was also a chance of meeting other POWs travelling, and exchanging a few bits of news, but we were never able to gather anything about how the war was going, except that America had now joined the Allies, and this had made us more hopeful. We had heard nothing about Pearl Harbor at that time.

Returning to Stalag 18A like a lost penny, on this occasion I did not report sick, and fell into the background and routine without being noticed.

We had an unexpected visit from a party of high-ranking German officers who were accompanied by British POWs dressed in German uniforms, with Union Jacks on their lapels. We felt this was quite disgusting, and to us they were real traitors. They were all recruiting for the German army and we were all ordered to go to a meeting where they spoke to us and handed out leaflets. We were told by them that if we joined the German army, we would be on the winning side, and they would give us a wonderful time in Berlin, where we would be accommodated in top-class hotels and be entertained with good food, wine and women.

When one of these British conscripts had to visit the toilets, two Aussies followed him and threw him into the stinking pit. He had to be pulled out, looking very sorry for himself, and smelling to high heaven. No one volunteered to join the German army from Stalag 18A. Although we were prisoners-of-war, we were still patriotic to our country.

Some Aussies made a still, and produced wood-alcohol. One of them must have had too much of it to drink, because it caused him to go blind, but I believe he got over it after a time. It must have been pretty lethal stuff!

After I left Stalag 18A for another working camp, I heard that a gang of POWs were trying to make a tunnel and took so many nails and wood from the inside of the building that it eventually collapsed. They had also removed the electric wiring. There would have been drastic punishments for this, and I was very glad I wasn't there when it happened.

If anyone stayed too long in a Stalag, the Germans were losing their forced labour, so they kept us moving, and very soon I was off to another working camp. I always seemed to have a bad reputation, but to be fair this was true, and I was intentionally a poor worker. I didn't want to help their war-effort.

Chapter Fifteen

This was now the summer of 1943, when I was sent off to a timber camp at a small hamlet called Gröss-Goërsgraben, which was about five miles into the foothills of the mountains. It was in the Kaiser Valley near Kufstein, which nowadays is a very much visited holiday area of considerable scenic beauty. Our nearest town was Leoban in Steiermark.

This was a heavy-duty timber camp, and I wondered what I was in for this time. We were turned out every morning at 6 am and worked until 6 pm with about half-an-hour for a snack at midday, which of course was out of our Red Cross parcels. Our ration as POWs was about half that of the civilians.

To get to our work, which was tree-felling, we had to walk about five miles or more up the lower foothills of the mountains. Civilian workers often lived on the job, in cabins they built from logs, with a hole in the roof to let out the smoke from the fire. We were allowed to go inside a cabin for our midday meal if the weather was bad. If it was windy, the smoke would blow back and you couldn't see across the cabin, and everybody would be choking and coughing.

Before we started work, trees would be marked out for felling by our civilian boss, Herr Lachmier. He was a huge Austrian with leathery features, and his son looked exactly like him. He was a very accomplished woodsman, and would sharpen our axes like razors. He also sharpened the cross-cut saws, a very expert job, and he would run a needle down between the points of the saw to make sure they were in perfect alignment. He was a very fair man to work for and secretly we quite admired him.

During his midday break, after Herr Lachmier had finished his usual piece of bread and speck, which was a very fatty pig-meat, he would immediately drop off to sleep. We would all keep very quiet, hoping that he would sleep long enough to give us a good rest, but as soon as the half-hour was up he would wake up like clockwork and order us out.

Our work was to go into the forest of very tall pine trees, where the tallest ones were felled and the smaller ones left standing to grow further. As we were under thick canopies of branches most of the time, we did not see much sunlight, and it was very miserable when it was cold and wet.

When sawing the trees down, we were paired off with an experienced civilian worker, who naturally did not appreciate our inexpert efforts and we came in for a lot of abuse most of which we could not understand. They could usually gauge exactly where a tree would fall, but on occasions it would twist as it fell and could easily kill or injure any worker underneath. I thought to myself, 'No wonder it's called a heavy-duty camp'. The saws were so sharp that you could hear them singing as they cut through the trees.

Our next job was to cut off the branches and then saw the tree trunks into the sizes required. The bark then had to be stripped off, and this was a rotten job as the sap would shoot out and by the end of the day our clothes would be as stiff as boards and sticky. When we took off our clothes at night, they would stand up by themselves. The bark was made into piles and at the end of the day we had to drag them down the mountainside to the nearest road, where they would be taken away by a horse and cart. This could be a tricky and dangerous job, especially at night or when it was dark.

During the summer, when working on a steep slope, the logs being slippery with sap would be shot off down the mountainside with the aid of tools called 'sapiens', which looked like half a pickaxe and had a special kind of groove at the end which could be stabbed into a log, and this enabled us to pull the log along without it slipping away. We also had to wear irons attached to our boots for walking over the logs. As our boots had been repaired with wooden strips across the soles, this made it very hard for walking.

When the logs were shot down the mountain and sometimes hit a tree head on, they would split down the middle and shoot out in all directions. It was very dangerous work even in the summer, and I was dreading the winter coming on. Most of us had very nasty cuts in our legs from the sharp axes. To get to a doctor or hospital with a serious accident, we had to make our coats into a stretcher and four men would then have to carry the injured man down the mountainside and along the road, probably about ten miles before help could be reached. One of our men had a splinter in his eye, and was in agony all the way to a hospital. They were very good there and managed to save his sight.

In the summertime, it was very hot and airless under the trees but very often there would be a fierce thunderstorm and the lightning would be dancing over the trees, bringing some crashing down. Then we had to run for our lives.

We were all sitting in the small log hut one day when there was a storm raging, having our midday bite, when Herr Lachmier shouted, Aus, aus!' We all rushed out just in time as a tall tree crashed through the roof. How he knew where it was going to fall we would never know. He must have had an extra sense in the woods, as he could always pull a few stones away and find a small spring of drinking water.

When winter came upon us, it was extremely cold and working outside was even harder and more dangerous. We now had to wear the iron spikes on our boots continually for walking over the icy ground and the logs. This was my third winter, and each one seemed worse than the last, as our clothes were not suitable for this kind of weather. They were always wet, even when we put them on in the morning. We still only had the allocated two thin blankets and still slept with our overcoats on top.

In the winter, we made an icy slide for the logs to shoot down the mountainside, and they would pile up at the bottom of the slope in a huge heap, sometimes 100 feet or more in height. The most dangerous time was when the logs were frozen and covered with snow. We had to go in amongst them to move them one by one without disturbing the top ones; if that happened you could be crushed to death by the top logs slipping, so we had to be very careful.

The slides we made were about 100 yards long, made by three logs clamped together and doused with water from a mountain stream which then froze. The logs were then placed on the chute, and when they started to slide we had to keep well out of the way. After they reached the bottom we had to load them into wagons, which were drawn by four or six large stallions. As it was nearly all downhill they could pull a very heavy load.

Once I was given the job of holding one of the stallions. He was a huge beast and looked round at me with an arrogant look, as if to say 'I'll show you who's the master!'. Then he took off like a rocket, taking me with him hanging on desperately to his bridle. I hung on for about twenty yards with my feet off the ground, then I let him go. Both the civilian and the guard were swearing at me in disgust, but this was the first time in my city life that I had had any contact with a horse. It took quite a long time to recapture him.

When the snow was very deep we had to go out and feed the deer and sometimes dig them out of the snow. Their stomachs were resting on the snow and their legs could not reach the ground to walk to their feeding place.

When any dangerous logging was in progress, the horses were always taken to a safe place, as they were far more important than the workers.

We had one lorry that was used on the occasions when it worked – it was run on wood-gas, and the engine was started on one small bottle of petrol, which was the whole of the ration for the day. One of us had to stand at the rear of the driver's cabin, where there was a dustbin contraption, and we had to feed small pieces of wood into the fire at the base of the bin. If we let the fire out we were in trouble.

We learned that, as we worked among the pine trees, they are very shallow rooted and easily blown over, when the whole flat roots would fly up out of the ground. When cutting at the base of a tree the large root, about ten feet in diameter, would fly back into the hole it had come out of. We always invited the German guard to stand in the root hole before it flew back, but he wasn't so daft.

Slim Hannan, my Aussie pal, on a very wet, cold day let his axe fly out of his grip whilst chopping off branches, and the axe missed my head by about two inches. My language was quite colourful on that occasion.

Another day when we were working, a large boulder as big as a room came hurtling down the mountainside and just missed us. We watched it crashing past us but could not see where it finished up.

Whilst working in the early summer alongside another comrade, there was a hornets' nest hanging from a tree and one of the branches he was chopping off disturbed the nest. I told him to run out of the way quickly but he assured me that hornets did not sting if you ignored them – but I ignored him and moved smartly away. He stayed where he was and the hornets attacked him and he was so badly stung he could hardly move for a week and nearly died from the pain of the stings.

Back at the camp one Sunday afternoon, I was busy outside cutting people's hair. The guard, who was a rather nice young chap, was watching, and I noticed his hair was getting long, so I offered to cut it for him. He propped his rifle up against the barbed wire and came and sat down on the chair, and I put a towel round his shoulders and started clipping away. Unfortunately, half-way through, the commandant arrived and gave him a good telling-off for leaving his rifle, which we could easily have taken. He was only a young Austrian, a village lad, who scarcely knew what war was about.

As we were loading a timber-carriage on a cold wet day, the civvy in charge was hoisting up one of the steel stanchions which held the logs together, but unfortunately did not put the holding bar in correctly, and the stanchion which weighed about half a hundredweight came down and hit him on the head with a crack. I thought he was dead when he fell over. I was very worried because I was on the top of the trailer when it happened, and as the guard the other side did not see what had happened, I thought I might have had the blame. However, it did not kill him, but he had to be taken to hospital with a large cut in his head. I couldn't believe it when he turned up for work next day and told the guard it was his own fault, which was a great relief to me. This chap was a typical mountain Austrian and, from what we could gather, he was no admirer of the Nazis.

Gradually the younger Austrians we had worked with began to disappear as they were called up for the army. I always got on well with the Austrians I met, as they always seemed honest, hard-working and decent people, and most must have had a very hard life in the mountains, without much contact with the outside world.

Chapter Sixteen

When taken out for work one morning, we were marched up to a small hamlet about five miles further up the valley. This was called Kleine-Goërsgraben, and was where our timber boss Herr Lachmier had a small guest house. We as usual made our way as slowly as we could, as the guard was behind us – when there was a guard in front we always had to go quicker.

The hamlet consisted of the guest house and three or four wooden houses clinging to the sides of a steep hillside. Herr Lachmier had a small apple orchard and made his own cider, which was renowned for being very strong. About six of us were given the job of picking the apples, which was all pleasure to us. We ate many ripe apples whilst doing the job, as they were a great delicacy for us, though we suffered afterwards, but it was worth it.

Herr Lachmier was a bit of a joker and took the guard off with him to give him a drink of his famous cider, then he slipped us a generous amount in a big stone jar. The outcome was that we were all very drunk, including the guard. We all rolled back to the camp very merry. On the way we met a smart horse-drawn carriage with a driver in front and a well-dressed lady and gentleman in the back. They turned out to be an Austrian count and countess and they spoke kindly to us in perfect English, but were obviously surprised and amused to see us all so merry. The countess said, in fun, 'You are not being very diligent today are you?' One of our more ignorant POWs retorted, in a drunken haze, 'We're just as bloody intelligent as you are!' We all fell about laughing, and even the guard laughed, though he had not the slightest idea what the joke was, nor had the man who said it.

When we got back to the camp, our commandant gave us all, including the guard, a real bawling out, and barred us from ever going there again. That day was at least one bright spot in four years.

On a Sunday afternoon we arranged a log-chopping contest between a Scotsman and a New Zealander. The Scot had been boasting about how expert he was, but little did he know that the New Zealander was a logger back home. They started off in good style but it wasn't long before the Scotsman was being left far behind and started to rush the job rather carelessly. He missed the log with his axe and cut right through his boot into his foot. He was lucky not to lose his toes and we had to carry him to hospital to have his foot stitched. It was no contest really, as the New Zealander was an expert. He told us that when back home out in the bush, he had cut his leg very badly with his axe, and had to sew it up himself with a needle and thread, then ride fifty miles on horseback to get to the nearest doctor.

It used to be a hard climb up into the mountains in the early morning and into the thick mist and clouds, then we would walk through the clouds and would see all the mountain peaks standing up all round. It was a magnificent sight such as tourists would go miles to see these days. Even in our circumstances we were aware of the marvellous scenery. Later in life I went back on holiday to try and find these places again, but never did. To somebody like me from the Black Country, it was really another most wonderful world.

After a day's work we were too tired to wash much, but we did have a bath in a wooden tub at weekends. Sometimes there was a little hot water which we shared out between us. There was also an ice-cold mountain stream nearby and we dammed it up as best we could and had a bit of a splash in that when it was summertime. It was melted snow, so was always terribly cold.

One of the civilians who worked with us was having a small house built and the builder was called up into the army and there was no one who could do the inside plastering. I got to hear of this and as we had a chap in the camp who boasted he was a master builder and could do any job in the building line I suggested to our camp commandant that he could do the necessary plastering thinking I was doing a good turn to our chap and the civvie, this latter who was quite a decent fellow.

This was agreed and the work went ahead. When the job was finished the guard took me in to see the finished work and to my horror all the walls and ceiling looked like the waves of the sea. Our so-called master builder never boasted again and it taught me never to volunteer information like that again.

In case anyone wonders why we elected to go out to working camps, only the sergeants and higher ranks were allowed to choose not to work. If anyone in the lower ranks refused to work, they had to sign a form and were then sent to a concentration camp, so we lower ranks went on working-parties and tried to do as little as possible. None of the work we did was supposed to be direct war work, which was as stated in the Geneva Convention.

I was feeling a bit fed up with all this heavy work and decided to try and think of a way of 'going sick', so that I could get back to the Stalag for a bit of a rest. The only excuse I could think of was that I had a cyst on my head, and although it never troubled me I rubbed and scratched it to make it look very angry. I then convinced the camp commandant that I should see the doctor. The doctor examined it, and told me that there would be a New Zealand surgeon visiting the small camps to do small operations and he would arrange for him to remove it, which was a nasty shock to me.

One Sunday afternoon, a few weeks later, the surgeon arrived and got out his tools. All the camp, including the guard, gathered round to see the fun. The surgeon made plenty of blood to impress the audience and put a nice lot of bandages round my head, and all the interested onlookers enjoyed themselves very much, but all I got was three days excused work – I didn't even get back to the Stalag.

We had a lot of trouble with fleas at this camp, and complained many times to our commandant, but he refused to accept that there were any in his camp, so we decided to prove it to him. When we had to go into his office to receive our pay, which was about three pfennigs a week (equivalent to a few coppers in our money), we each caught a flea and threw it on his bed, which was in the room. We thought that would prove our point, but we couldn't believe it when he still insisted there were no fleas – they must have been special fleas bred only to bite the British.

I noticed that when a man meets a lady in the more remote parts of Austria and are very friendly the man kisses the lady on both cheeks and then gives her a gentle tweak on her breasts which the lady appears to enjoy, as usually they give a little giggle. Makes one wonder what went on in these Austrian mountains.

In the small farmhouses in the mountains there always seemed to be very beautiful children and they were always most friendly. I don't think most of them had seen a German soldier let alone British soldiers. It was surprising how many children were called Hansel and Gretel. They all worked on the farm no matter how young, and always looked happy and contented.

We were surprised one day when the commandant handed us leaflets printed in English, which had been sent out by the German Propaganda Ministry to all POWs. This stated that the German army had broken through at Stalingrad and the war with Russia was almost won and Germany would be victorious. Of course we never knew what was really happening on the Russian Front, so this made us rather despondent, as rumours had circulated that the Allies were getting the upper hand. Later, of course, we heard that this was all lies, but when eventually the truth was that the Germans were being beaten in Russia, there were no leaflets handed out from Herr Goebbels then.

At this camp we had to do our own cooking on a small range. Our meat ration was very small and very often going 'off', but we were fortunate in having one man who had been a chef in one of the best hotels in London. He would prepare and cook the meat and make it taste palatable. He told us a lot of the meat he cooked in the London hotel was very often going off, but was always used up. That was at the beginning of the war and I expect things are much better now. He used to say thatpeople attending large banquets ate very little, and that it would be possible to put six courses on a saucer. If people complained about the food, the waiter took it back, turned it over, spat on it, and took it back again to a very satisfied customer. I think this story did actually have some truth in it.

We were lucky at this camp to have a Maori, as he could light a fire outside when we were working in all weathers. He would just pick up a few scraps from under a tree, strike a match, drop the lighted pieces to the ground and throw almost anything on top and in no time would have a good blaze going. Even the guard was impressed.

Later on in the year during the summer, we had a most wonderful day. We were working in a clearing of the trees on a mountainside, when we began to hear a deep humming noise, which gradually got louder and louder, and the whole mountainside seemed to be throbbing. We had no idea what it could be until suddenly we looked up and saw hundreds of four-engined bombers in a huge formation, flying slowly overhead leaving their white vapour-trails behind them. They moved round in a large circle and we reckoned there must have been 500 planes at least. Then, from another direction, there appeared another huge formation of about 500, and they all joined together, covering the sky with their vapour trails. They were too high up to see any markings, but we assumed they were American planes. It was an amazing and wonderful sight and we couldn't help giving a cheer before they moved off in the direction of Vienna. I shall never forget the expression of utter amazement on the guard's and civilians' faces.

We learned after that were going to bomb the big munition works in Wiener-Neustadt on the outskirts of Vienna. Whilst they were overhead, anti-aircraft flak was being fired at them from all directions and, as the planes were directly over our heads, the pieces of shrapnel were landing all round us. The noise was like a great organ playing. We tried to protect ourselves with pieces of bark held above our heads, but one elderly civvy could not believe what was going on and just stood there mesmerised, until a piece of shrapnel about a foot long, landed alongside the axe which he was holding and stuck into the log which he was working on. He soon tried to take cover like we had.

In that area, I don't think the locals had ever seen a plane before, much less a thousand all at once. They must have realised then that they were losing the war.

When we got back to the camp, the commandant looked very worried and told us his wife was living in Vienna.

That day was the happiest one for us in over three years.

Our usual entertainment in the evenings was playing cards as we had no books to read, but one night we were casting around for something else to amuse ourselves.

A chap who had come from Glasgow suddenly said, 'What about a bit of table-lifting?'

We looked at each other, and said, 'What the hell is that?'

'Well,' he said, 'my sister and I at home found out quite by accident that we could do spirit table-lifting quite easily. The way we found out was because we had a small table in our hall, and one day when we both put our hands on it at the same time, it lifted itself up on one leg. This gave us a bit of a shock, and we used to put some heavy books and a plant on it to keep it down.'

Of course, we thought this was a real joke, and ribbed him about it, until he said. 'OK, if you don't believe me, let's try it here.'

We gaped at him and said, 'You'll never lift this heavy old mess table.'

We were very scathing, but he made us sit around the table, four of us, and we placed our hands on the top. He told us to wait, and concentrate hard, and be quiet. We all sat looking at each other with silly smirks on our faces. 'How long have we got to wait for this miracle?' I said with a grin.

He told me to keep quiet and wait, 'It may happen any time, just keep concentrating.'

We sat still, looking at each other but feeling very silly, when suddenly the table beneath our hands gave a lurch. This startled us considerably and we accused each other of lifting it with our knees but all four of us denied this. It began to lift again very slowly and, however hard we tried, we could not push it down as long as our hands were on top.

A chap who was watching got quite scared and jumped onto his bunk and put his head under the blanket. We got another man to hold the oil lamp that we had underneath and put his hands under the legs of the table to make sure that there was a clear space between all four legs and the floor. At this moment, the poor old cat who used to come inside for a warm-up by the stove when he could, suddenly leaped up and shot out of the window between the bars. He looked scared to death.

For several nights there was great interest in this phenomenon, but one evening the guard looked in and saw what was going on and reported it to the camp commandant. He came storming in and ordered us to stop it at once. He told us that Hitler had personally banned all psychic practices. Although we learned later that Hitler was very much interested in spiritualism, he evidently did not want anyone else, especially his enemies, to be in on the act.

Actually, we never thought of ever asking any spirits a question, which I suppose we should have done. It might have given us a bit of information about the end of the war . . .

Chapter Seventeen

Slim Hannan, the Aussie, Cyril Winter and myself had become good pals in this timber camp. We all wanted to get away before winter set in, as this was a cold and dangerous job and we were getting fed up and felt we needed a change.

The only idea we could think of was to try to escape. We talked it over for a few weeks and put aside some food from our Red Cross parcels. Our pals at the camp had been kind enough to give us a few bits and pieces out of their parcels.

I must have been mad to think of escaping with Slim Hannan, who was the champion walker of the Australian army – in civvy street he was a bagman, that is one who travels around Australia following the sun and doing odd jobs. Cyril Winter was a big, powerful chap whilst I was half his size and not too strong. They told me if I couldn't keep up with them they wouldn't b— well carry me, but I hoped it wouldn't come to that.

We hoped that when we did escape, no reprisals would be taken against those left in the camp. One civilian we had to steer clear of was the local *jaeger*, (huntsman) as he would probably be told to keep an eye out for us. He was a crack shot with his rifle and as we had seen him shoot a fox on the run, we certainly did not fancy meeting him.

We had also been told by previous escapees to get well clear of the local area, as we would get a very warm reception from pals of our guards in the local barracks.

At last we decided to make our getaway. We had not long had a new camp commandant, who was a proper ladies' man, and he soon found a girl from the village with whom he could stay the night, so we made sure he was out with his girlfriend on the night we left, which was the 5 October 1944.

The day before we left, we hid some clothes and food in the woods where we were working, so we could pick them up after we had escaped from the camp. We went through the perimeter wire without any trouble when it was dusk and the guard was out of sight.

It was a fine night when we left, but very soon it started to snow, the first of the winter. We went up the hillside into the woods to pick up our bits and pieces but we were shocked to find how dark it was. In the forest at night it is pitch black and it was almost impossible to know what direction we were taking. We had no compass and seemed to be going round in circles. Slim had told us it was easy to find one's way in a forest as the moss on the treetrunks always grew on the north side, but these trees seemed to have moss on both sides and all round on others. We were hopeful of crossing the border into Yugoslavia but soon found out how ignorant and ill-informed we were.

After a few miles we decided we must rest, as we were completely lost, so we huddled together to try and keep warm, and tried to catch a bit of sleep. We felt a cold wind striking us in our faces and I felt that something was not quite right and we were in danger. It was a good thing that we had not gone any further, as when daylight came, we found ourselves right on the edge of a precipice, and if we have gone another few steps we would either have been injured or killed as the next stop was a long way down.

As we moved on, we kept to the mountains where possible, but had to descend when we could see no possible way onward, then we had to get onto a road. Evening was drawing in by this time, and everything seemed very quiet, so we walked along it for a few miles.

It was getting darker now, but a moon was coming up which shed a soft hazy light, enough to see our way by. As we were walking along, we suddenly heard the clip-clop of a horse's hooves which seemed to be approaching from behind us, and the sight of a horseman coming towards us made us stop in our tracks. I said to Slim, 'It's no good trying to hide now as he's already seen us,' so we stood where we were and watched him approach expecting to be challenged at any moment. To us he looked like either a policeman or a soldier, with a dark uniform and a tall round-topped hat. This was a uniform that we had never seen before, and he had a holster on the horse's saddle with a revolver poking out of it. Then the strangest thing happened – he came almost alongside us but never spoke or appeared to see us, although we were in the middle of the road and right in his way. We were still waiting to be arrested and marched back at gunpoint, when he slowly turned the horse round and cantered off into the misty moonlight. His face was in the shadows so we could not see his features.

We stood looking at each other in amazement, open-mouthed. This seemed very strange to us, as an armed German would certainly never let three men go free who were obviously POWs in British army uniforms.

Slim said, 'He must have seen us, so why didn't he arrest us?'

There were no houses or farms along the road as we came, and the village in that direction must have been more than ten miles away. We had never seen a mounted policeman, or that kind of uniform before in Austria. We kept asking ourselves where could he be going and why did he ignore us, and in any case where did he come from. Some time later, when we were talking about it, we wondered if he could have been a ghost rider. Later in life, I saw the picture of a similar uniform in an old book of military uniforms, which were from the last century . . . I am quite sure now that we were actually visited by a ghost.

After this strange experience we left the road and made for the woods again to try and get a bit of rest. The next morning, after a very cold night with snow on the ground, we headed down the road towards the village we could see in the distance. We soon found out that there was no way to get around this village, as it was between high cliffs with a mountain stream on one side and a big timber works on the other. We decided to take a chance of walking through the village as it was quite early in the morning. However, we reckoned without a small crowd of children who were going to school.

There were no grown-ups to be seen, and when the children caught sight of us they ran towards us chattering and laughing as children will, then they tried to hold our hands and were asking who we were, and where had we come from. We told them we were two Englishmen and one Australian, and they seemed very interested in the Australian as they had never seen one before.

As we walked through the village, accompanied by the children, a police station came into sight, and we felt sure the children would be running in to tell the police they had caught some prisoners, but instead of that they held their fingers to their lips as if to say, 'Keep quiet!' I don't think the policeman could have been very popular with the children.

We thought this could be the end of our escape, as we all stopped outside the police station and looked in through the window, and saw two policemen talking together.

They seemed to be reading a paper of some sort. It would have been interesting to know if it had contained news of three escaped prisoners of war believed to be in that area, and we were not even three yards away from them. They did not see us, so we carried on with the crowd of children right to the end of the village, where they wished us goodbye and ran off to school looking very pleased with themselves.

We then went into the woods again, and found a clear cold mountain stream, where we had a drink of water and had a wash. We had used up all our small stock of food by this time. It was not possible to store up any food for escaping as the guards always did a search of our bunks when we were out working.

The next night we spent on the higher slopes of the mountain. We were amazed to come across three Italian soldiers, who were probably deserters trying to make their way home. They were very friendly, and showed us how to make a very comfortable bed out of the lower pine branches, they had obviously done this before as they were quite experts. We did not have a very peaceful night, however, as the mountain deer were running around and jumping right over us, but not one actually jumped upon us, thank goodness. The next morning, when we woke up, the Italians had gone.

We trudged along the mountainsides for two more days, getting colder and hungrier as it began to snow again, and Slim said, 'Which of you idiots suggested this escape madness?' It had been him, but we didn't say anything.

The next night saw the end of our escapade but at least we had been free for six nights and days. Our boots were nearly worn through and our clothes were wet through and we felt ready to be recaptured. We had no food left, and the Yugoslav border was as far away as ever. It would take better men than we were to find our way over these mountains.

Chapter Eighteen

After leaving the village where we saw the children we again headed for the mountains, but got so tired and, seeming to get nowhere, we decided to take our chance on the narrow country road, which seemed very quiet with no traffic. We had no idea what the village was called.

We trudged on steadily for a time, seeing nobody, but then, as we crossed a narrow bridge, we ran straight into a group of three Brownshirts (civilian SS) carrying machine pistols. I think they had been waiting all through the war to arrest somebody and seemed absolutely delighted to see us. They arrested us immediately and ordered us to put our hands above our heads, then they marched us along the road towards the next village.

They would not allow anything to pass us on the road and a lorry coming up behind us was ordered to follow us and keep his headlights on. Even cyclists had to dismount and follow us on foot. We were soon heading a small parade, probably enjoyed by everyone except us. We were in no state to put up any resistance anyway, as we were just about all in.

We started to sing 'Roll Out the Barrel', and got poked hard in the back by their guns, probably they did not think much of our singing voices.

When we eventually reached a guest house in the village, one of the Brownshirts ordered all the civvies out and ushered us in, then ordered us to sit down in the far corner of the room. Two of them guarded the doors, with their machine pistols at the ready, and the third was sent off presumably for reinforcements.

In the guest house was a middle-aged lady and two pretty young ladies, and we learned that she was the proprietor and her daughters. The lady was doing her ironing and the two daughters were standing behind the bar which ran along one side of the room. When things had quietened down a bit, Cyril, in his usual jocular fashion, called to the girls, *Drei Bier, bitte!*' As one of the girls reached for the glasses our guards saw red at this and shouted, *'Ruhe, ruhe,'* ('quiet, quiet') and pointed their pistols at us in a threatening manner. The girl nearly dropped the glasses, they both screamed and hid their faces in their hands and their mother started to cry.

The mother looked at us very sympathetically and I suppose she thought we looked a bit rough and could do with a feed. The two girls were soon back to normal and I think enjoying the excitement, as they would not leave the room even after the guards had ordered them out; they weren't going to miss anything, it was probably the best real-life drama they had seen for a long time in that quiet village. I had the feeling that the three sharp fellows who had caught us were not very popular with anybody.

After an interval, the third Brownshirt brought in the chief of police and the commandant of a nearby camp. We had quite a shock when they came towards us, shook our hands, and sat down and ordered coffee and bread. The first thing they asked was, 'Which one of you is the Australian?' So we knew then they were looking for us. He ordered the somewhat subdued Brownshirts to put their guns away and sit down on the other side of the room.

The commandant told us he had a son who was a POW in England, and he was very worried about him. We assured him he would be well treated, which pleased him very much. We then had a nice chat with everybody there, except the three Brownshirts, who looked a bit crestfallen. They did cheer up when the commandant brought out some forms and took the particulars of all three, including their wives and children. They probably thought then that they would be getting a medal.

Afterwards, we were escorted to the dirtiest and most dismal gaol imaginable, for which the police chief apologised. When he closed the door on us, the lights went out and we were left in pitch darkness, and had to feel around to try and find somewhere to sleep. When, next morning, we saw the blankets we had pulled round us, they were filthy and covered with blood.

Next day a military guard called for us and escorted us to the local station. He was quite a pleasant sort of chap and told us it would be a long journey to the other side of Austria, to the Tyrol.

It was a rule that any prisoners were not allowed any food or drink until they got to their destination, but fortunately we met some Aussies on the train and were put in the same carriage. They had some food with them and the guard allowed them to give us what they could spare and, as we were very hungry we were grateful for it.

Our next bit of luck was at Klagenfurt Station where there was a soup kitchen for the German troops passing through. Our guard, who really was a decent chap, allowed us to take our cocoa tins and join the queue; we never lost sight of our cocoa tins, in case anything would turn up. Before anyone who was dishing out the soup realised who we were, our tins had been filled, and our guard had some too.

Towards the evening, we arrived at Landeck Station and were marched up to Landeck Castle, which was a thirteenth-century fortress, standing on a small hill above the town. Later in life I was to see it again from the train as my wife and I were going on holiday to the Tyrol.

When we arrived at the castle, we were first searched, then escorted to separate cells for solitary confinement.

The cells were like small dungeons, with a tiny barred window high up on the wall, about a foot square, and which let in very little light. The sleeping arrangement was a wooden board, with no pillow or blanket, and the toilet was a bucket. It was very cold and damp, as it was now the end of October.

Next morning, we were each taken separately to be interrogated by a Nazi officer, who spoke good English. He was very arrogant, exquisitely turned out and smoking a cigarette in a long holder, and also had a monocle. There could not have been a bigger contrast in dress between two people facing each other. His black leather jacket shone and he had an Iron Cross hanging round his neck on a ribbon, also I noticed he was smelling strongly of perfume.

My own impression of him was that the was dressed up and smelt 'like a pox-doctor's clerk' as the army expression goes.

He seemed a right pig, and shouted at me, 'Vy did you try to escape?' I told him I thought it was my duty to try, at which he looked very grim. Then I had a sudden inspiration to try a bit of bull, and said to him, 'If you were a POW in England, wouldn't you have done the same?'

He agreed and said, 'I would have done a better job than you!' Then he thumped the desk and laughed his head off, and yelled to the guard to take me back to my cell.

Later in the morning I was picked out by the guard to go round all the cells with him, handing out the bread and water, but I was given strict orders that I must not speak to anybody.

I saw prisoners of various nationalities, probably about fifty in number, all in solitary confinement. One British officer had a cell with a doorway, which led out onto a battlement, where he could have a short walk.

After about a week we were allowed to join others in a larger room, and there were about twenty of us altogether. All were escapees waiting to go to their respective Stalags to serve their time in gaol.

Whilst there, I had the doubtful pleasure of playing bridge with a Russian, a Pole and a Frenchman. My partner was the Russian who I think was an officer. His uniform was very ragged but he reminded me of Rasputin as he had a large black beard and staring eyes and looked very fierce. The Frenchman was a youngish man, but very quiet and with a worried look. As far as I could gather he had been caught with an Austrian girl.

The Pole was a civvie and had got away from a working party. The Poles hated the Russians as much as the Germans, which was understandable, as they were treated badly by both sides.

The bidding was rather like the Mad Hatter's Tea Party, each trying to make each other understand the different suits and the bidding. My partner the Russian, insisted that we won, but it really made no difference, as none of us had any money. The pack of cards we used was so badly worn that the pictures were hardly visible.

Two Aussies were let out of solitary confinement and joined us. They had escaped from a working camp and told us they had got very near to the Hungarian border, but had then been captured by a farmer when he caught them sleeping in his barn. The farmer must have panicked and fired a shot-gun straight at them. They were both peppered with shot, and you could see the black dots all over them. They were still in pain, but the Germans would do nothing about it. We were told it was a dangerous game escaping, and this certainly proved it.

In about two weeks, Slim Hannan, Cyril Winter and myself were taken overnight to another camp – I never was able to find out the name of it – it seemed to be specially for escaped prisoners. One night we were woken up by the sound of hundreds of men being brought in, and we found out later they were our own men who had been captured at the Battle of Arnhem. We were never allowed out here, so we could not speak to them and get any news.

In the bunkhouse where we were held, there were two Americans, I think they were airmen, but they did not speak to anybody. They had got a food parcel from somewhere and were eating the contents while hidden under the blankets. I suppose this was understandable, as there would have been too many men to share with.

Soon after this we were taken back to Stalag 18A and were put into another section of that camp which was for real, tough, POWs, those who had refused to work, and those who had been mixing with Austrian women, as well as escapees. Most were men who were going to be sent on to a concentration camp, though we had not heard that word used before.

They were mostly tough Aussies who would have made John Wayne look like a 'patsy'. You dared not even take your boots off or any clothing when you slept at night or they would be gone next morning. We were told that some men would break their fingers and one had even got his friends to break his arm, so that he would not be sent on to the next camp. The guards never entered this compound, but left the food at the gate.

I was never so pleased in my life as to get out of that place. Slim Hannan was a great help to us two Englishmen, as he was very tough and could give the other Aussies as good as anything they could dish out.

We were later transferred to do our three-week sentence for escaping and put into the main gaol of the camp. Our meal consisted of bread and water with thin soup on the third day.

The cell I was in was very well decorated – the POW who had done this must have been a first-class artist. It was all pictures in coloured chalks, the walls, ceiling and door were all covered in naked ladies and cherubs. It was rather like a baroque church interior, except that the ladies were no angels. One thing which struck me as being very comical, was that the small hole in the door where the guard put his eye to check up on us, was right between the top of the legs of a rather buxom lady nude.

We were not allowed to smoke but if you had a friend outside in the main camp he would throw a few cigarettes over the wire when the guard was not looking. Luckily Slim did have a friend outside who threw some over to us.

Every morning we were searched and turned out into the corridor. I always managed to beat the guards by smoking after they had searched us as, when they frisked us down, they never looked into our hands. It gave us great pleasure to be caught smoking after the search. They never did find out how we had hoodwinked them.

Chapter Nineteen

We were returned to the main Stalag after three weeks in gaol. I was feeling fed up one morning, and decided to stay in my bunk instead of going on roll-call, and when the guard came round to check I would plead sickness. When everybody was out on parade, the guard came in to check up and saw me in my bunk and ordered me out. I told him I was sick and couldn't walk. He then fixed his bayonet and poked me in the backside with it. Realising he meant business, I jumped out of my bunk and ran. He chased me round the parade ground, still trying to give me a poke. I had no trousers on and with my shirt tails flying, I raced through the snow bare-footed, being cheered on by all the POWs on parade, and also the guards.

I fell in between the ranks and all were highly amused. They kept me standing there for a long time while my feet and behind were getting almost frozen. I didn't try that again.

News was getting round the camp that there was to be an exchange of sick POWs with German POWs in England. All sorts of ideas were being thought out as to how to hoodwink the German doctors. One idea was to swallow small pieces of silver paper and complain of stomach ulcers, as somebody had said they would show up on an X-Ray. A few tried this, but never got away with it.

One man complained of severe pains in his right side, and the doctor diagnosed appendicitis. He was sent into hospital to have his appendix out, but when they cut him open they found it was already gone.

An Aussie who seemed a bit simple said his neck was broken

and went round holding his head on one side. The doctor sent him packing and, as he had held it on one side for so long, he had to get his pals to massage it to get it back straight again.

Stone-deafness was another ploy, and one man managed to fool them right to the end. He passed all the tests, including having heavy weights dropped behind him; also a piano was played, making bangs and terrible noises, they shouted and bawled at him behind his back and he never turned a hair. When he was called into the office to get his repatriation papers and was leaving the room feeling very pleased with himself, the officer called to him, 'Have a good journey!' He turned around and said 'Thank you very much'. That finished him.

I agreed to go back to a working camp, and was sent to Steinach-in-Erding, which is about fifty miles from Salzburg. Moving about was a fact of life for me at that time. No sooner had I settled in one camp and made friends, than I was sent off again. However, I was not displeased at moving as one always thought the next stop would be better than the last, but sometimes it was worse, and of course I lost touch with many of the pals I had made. I was glad that Slim and Cyril were also transferred with me to Steinach.

Our first task was to help build a milk factory. I often wonder if it is still standing, as we put lots of blocks of ice and snow into the foundations, as it was in the depths of winter again by this time.

On the way back from work, we would often pass a row of milk churns at the old factory, and if we were close enough the man on the outside rank would grab one and pass it to the man in the middle rank, who would put his overcoat over it and smuggle it into the camp. Next morning, we would return the empty in the same way, which was very thoughtful of us. Funnily enough, we were never found out.

The weather began to get much colder and the Red Cross parcels were not getting through, except for the odd one. After a relatively quiet time building the milk factory, things were now taking a different turn and we wondered what was going on. Trains started to pass through the station full of troops who looked battle-weary, and we wondered if there had been a big retreat somewhere or were they moving troops from the Western to the Eastern Front, as that was the direction they were taking.

Very soon American planes saw what was happening at the station and on the railway lines, and we had regular visits from the bombers and cannon-firing fighters. Our job was now switched to filling in bomb craters – and as soon as we filled in one lot they came and made more. Bombing and strafing was very regular now where we were working and unfortunately one of our chaps was killed.

Many railway engines were hit and steam and water escaped from the holes made by the cannon fire. Troop trains would come through every day now, and we had to keep our heads down and look busy as they looked ready to shoot anybody in British uniform.

Once we saw the camouflage netting fall off one of the coaches of the troop train and four German soldiers were sent up on top of the coach to put it back on again. One of them accidentally touched the overhead electric cables of 40,000 volts, there was a terrific flash and fire broke out. Two of the men fell off apparently dead, and the other two had to be taken down screaming in pain to be taken off by ambulance. We were close to them when it happened, and it showed how dangerous the work could be if anything touched the wires.

I myself had once touched one of the wires with a long metal pole when working on a siding, but the signalman had turned the electricity off as there were no trains running along that line at the time, so I was very lucky.

We heard that an American plane had been shot down over a mountain nearby called Grimming, and everybody in the local village was full of amazement as there were black men in it, and they had never seen any before.

I was working with three other men filling in bomb craters on the railway line, which was a single line between Steinach and Bad Aussee. The four of us, with a guard, had a small trolley propelled on the line by pushing a handle up and down. We enjoyed going on this, as we could get up a good speed, especially on the downward slopes. The guard had to collect a staff to make sure the line would be clear, and we had to report to the signalman at our destination.

One day while we were having our short midday break inside the signalbox, an American cannon-firing fighter made an attack on the station. He hit the box but did very little damage and we ran out across a field. The plane circled to come back towards us, so we hurriedly scraped out a rough Union Jack in the snow with our boots and waved our arms like mad. He must have seen us, because he dipped his wings and flew off.

On another occasion, going at speed on our rail trolley, we were attacked again by a plane, but he missed us. That was another American. We did not know whether to go faster or jump off; at that time in the war the American planes had complete mastery of the skies.

Our guard, who was an oldish man, who was sitting on the back of the trolley, looked very scared. We seemed to be getting older men or those who had been wounded at the Front for our guards now.

A lot of damage was done on that part of the track between Steinach, Bad Aussee and Bad Ischl. I did not know then that the old Austrian Emperor, Franz Joseph, had a summer palace at Bad Ischl and that I would visit it in the future after the war.

From Steinach, a rack and pinion railway ran up the mountain through very magnificent scenery to a remote village called Donnersbach, where we had to do repairs to the railway line. Once, coming downhill out of a tunnel, an American Bulldog plane saw the engine and started to attack with his cannons. The driver quickly stopped the train and reversed back into the tunnel, and we stayed there until the plane gave up and went away.

The mountains around here were probably six or seven thousand feet high and the people who lived in these remote areas had scarcely known there was a war on until these last few weeks. This place looked very beautiful in the snow, just like we had seen on Christmas cards.

One small hamlet we passed in the train had a small church, and underneath was the charnel house, which was so full of bones that they were overflowing out of the crypt onto the ground outside. Several of the churches in Austria were on such rocky ground that it was impossible to find space for many graves, so the usual practice was to dig up the old ones, throw the bones in the crypt and re-use the graves. Hallstadt, now a famous tourist place, is a good example of this, where the bones are painted to denote the sex and age of the persons.

Among the mountains, too, there were little shrines dotted everywhere, for which we were very grateful, as we often used them for shelter during the rain and very heavy thunderstorms which used to come up suddenly in the mountains, but we were never allowed to stop work just for snow.

As Austria is a mainly Catholic country, the churches and shrines are beautifully maintained and decorated, even in the poorest areas. The people were usually very religious and always greeted anybody with '*Gruss Gott.*' The priests had an easy job as all they used to do was to walk round the houses and bless them, then collect money from the poor occupants.

I had really fallen in love with Austria, in spite of our privations, and hoped to be able to visit it again, and this did come to pass in the future.

When we were working one day a terrible blizzard was blowing, and we could hardly stand up, and as we knew now that the war was coming to an end, we were feeling very brave and cheeky, so refused to work. The guard then marched us to the local barracks, probably to be put in gaol as usual. I was chosen to go in front of the commandant as spokesman, and he had with him a very beautiful French lady to act as interpreter. I explained that the weather was so bad that we could not see to work, or even stand up, but I had to agree to go back to work as he told us the SS were in the district and they would not hesitate to shoot us.

We were then marched away by our guard, and was being congratulated by the rest of the gang for getting them off gaol, but just as we reached the gates of the barracks we were stopped, turned round, and marched right back again, and into the gaol for seven days. My popularity did not last long – back to bread and water and thin soup.

We were put in a large room all together, with heavy bars on the windows, and the guards just brought our usual food every day but never spoke to us. Down the corridor from us there was a row of small cells, and we often heard crying and shouting coming from some of them, and we wondered what was going on, as it seemed to be nearing the end of the war.

When at last we came out, and arrived back at our working camp, the camp commandant told us it looked as if the war would soon be over, and not to take any more chances. He said there was a lot of talk going on that the Allies and the Germans should unite and fight the Russians, as they were the greatest menace. This was a great surprise to us and we thought it very unlikely.

The next Sunday afternoon a guard came in and ordered six of us to accompany him outside, and all six being part of the gang which had been in gaol, I thought this was it, as we had already been threatened with the SS for going on strike. The guard led us off, and to our absolute astonishment we were taken into the town and into the local cinema. We realised then that they knew that the end of the war was in sight.

Soon after this, fourteen men from our camp were taken away as hostages, and my friend Slim the Aussie was one of these men. Luckily for me I was not chosen, as we heard afterwards that they had had a very rough time and the only food they had was what they could scrounge on the march. They had to march very long distances, and we never found out where they went.

The guard told us this was happening to British POWs all over Germany. I did not see Slim again until we eventually met up on repatriation leave and he never told me the full story, but I believe it was very harrowing.

There was a lot of bombing still going on and the fourteen of us that were left had to go on filling in the bomb craters. American planes were coming over and dropping bombs at regular intervals.

We had heard rumours that the Russians were getting very

near, and the local people seemed to be more afraid of the Russians than they were of the Americans as the latter were known to be kind-hearted and better disciplined, whereas they regarded the Russians as barbarians.

We were wondering now what had happened to Hitler and his gang, but we were never told anything. I think that was one of the worst aspects of being a prisoner, we never knew anything about what was going on.

Food was now shorter than ever as no Red Cross parcels were getting through due to the chaos on the railway. The loaves of black bread we were now receiving were getting smaller and smaller, and were now about half the size of what they had been, and they were never large. They still had to be divided up the same as before. The guard told us that the civilians were suffering just as much as we were and they were very short of food too.

We felt we were living from day to day now and wondered how soon the war would end.

Chapter Twenty

One morning we were awakened early by the sound of heavy gunfire and we thought we were in the middle of a battle. I rushed to the barred window to look out and try and find out what was going on, and I saw one of our guards in civilian clothes, with the guard dog on a lead, walking out of the camp. Then I saw the other guards also leaving and the perimeter gate was open.

I turned to my pals and shouted, 'This must be the end of the war! It looks as if they are all leaving!'

We threw on our clothes hurriedly, and rushed out of the billet door, which had been left unlocked, and ran out to see what all the gunfire was about. We found we were surrounded with what looked like the whole of the German army and the gunfire was from their heavy guns being spiked.

Cyril Winter and myself with one other chap, walked out of the camp and into the town. We were amazed to see so many high-ranking German officers, most of them looking like the SS in their leather coats, all standing round talking and looking very miserable. They took no notice of us whatsoever, and I thought how strange it was to be walking about free among so many German officers.

One sight I remember clearly because it struck me as comical, was that coming down the road was a large chauffeur-driven limousine with two generals sitting in the back smoking their cigars and not looking over-worried, while they were being drawn along by two oxen. The car had evidently run out of fuel. It looked quite a come-down for them.

The local tobacconist, who had always given us a friendly

nod, suddenly rushed out of his shop crying, 'Churchill on the radio!'

He grabbed us excitedly by the arms and pulled us into his shop, and then he invited us into his living room where the radio was on, and he said, 'Mr Churchill is going to make a speech.'

We listened delightedly to the sound of Big Ben striking – the first time we had heard that for many years. Then Mr Churchill's voice came through telling us the wonderful news that the Germans were defeated and the war was over. We knew that the tobacconist was no Nazi, and he was just as pleased as we were. We then were all given a drink of schnapps to celebrate.

The whole town of Steinach was absolutely full of German troops and the roads were blocked with tanks and armoured vehicles. Everybody except us was looking very worried.

We realised that we had got to get out of the area as quickly as possible, as the Russians were not far away. We found out afterwards that even the British prisoners were treated very badly by the Russians. We could see in the distance a narrow track which was full of a long line of civilians pushing their belongings on trucks, prams, and even wheelbarrows, all trying to get away from the Russian Front. They trusted the Americans, but hated the thought of being captured by the Russians.

While we had been listening to Mr Churchill, our other colleagues had been down to the railway station and had found a small consignment of Red Cross parcels in a shed. With these parcels we were able to bribe a local haulier to take us in his small coach through to the American lines, as our main objective now was to get through the German lines to reach the Allies. Some of the German soldiers still appeared to be belligerent towards us as we tried to drive through. At first it seemed to be impossible to move far, but we managed to get the help of a German officer, who stood on the running-board shouting and ordering all the lorries and tanks to get out of the way.

The journey was very slow and still took a long time, but without his help I don't think we would have ever got through.

His assistance was not entirely disinterested as he wanted to get to the American lines and give himself up to be under their protection.

After being ordered about and shouted at for four years by the Germans, it was highly amusing, not to say unbelievable, for us fourteen scruffy POWs to see the German tanks, guns, armoured cars, officers and troops ordered by our own attendant officer to get out of the way and allow us to go by. The German troops didn't look too pleased about it either.

The officer with us rode on the running-board of our bus waving his arms and shouting and for the first and only time in our lives we felt like real VIPs.

We realised in retrospect that if the war had not ended on that day we would probably have been bombarded by the Americans on one side and the Russians on the other, as they were only about twenty miles away on either side of us.

As we got near the American lines, we saw truck loads of American infantry lined up, complete with heavy guns and tanks. It was a marvellous sight to see the Germans piling up their arms and being ordered about by the Americans.

The Americans lived up to their usual kindness and gave us food right away – a tin of biscuits, a tin of peaches and a tin of bacon – the best meal we had seen for over four years. We realised then that we were truly free at last.

As they took us into their care, we were given regular meals and as much as we could eat. The irony of it was that it was being ladled out by German POWs who looked very fat and full.

After what the Americans did for our country I cannot understand how people can criticise them, I shall always be very grateful towards them.

It was amazing to us to see the casual way the Americans left their guns – one of them had a machine-gun on a jeep and he just threw a rug over it and walked away and left it.

One POW who was watching the Germans piling up their arms, picked up a revolver and started to play about with it, and accidentally shot himself. It was unfortunate after spending all that time as a prisoner.

113

We walked into a nearby village, where the Americans had taken over a small bakery and were having white bread baked. We stood outside, breathing in the beautiful aroma. After the horrible soggy black stuff we had been having, we were looking forward to having real white bread again.

After a few days we were taken by lorry to a small aerodrome to be flown to France in a Dakota. As we were about to take off, one of the engines caught fire, and we were all told to get out as quickly as possible. The Americans seemed quite casual about this and said it was nothing unusual. They pushed it off the runway and we got into another one.

We arrived in France, at a big American camp. We were called into a tent and some medical orderlies searched through our hair for livestock and went through our clothes for lice, and we then had some powder puffed all over us. We were all absolutely lousy but had got so used to it that we were getting immune to the bites. We then had a shower with real soap, which was a wonderful treat, and as we came out of the shower we were fitted out with American army uniforms, which felt luxurious compared to our rough, worn-out attire.

We were then sent onto the aerodrome again, to be taken over to England. After a very long wait we were led off to a Wellington bomber, and about forty of us were piled in, each being given a number and told to find that number in the plane and sit on that spot, no matter how uncomfortable, and not move, or it would throw the plane out of balance.

We landed after about an hour's flight on a south coast aerodrome, and then I was put on a train for Birmingham. I cannot express how good it felt to be on English soil again.

At Birmingham station, there were lines of cars run by volunteers waiting to pick up all ex-POWs and take them to their homes.

When I walked in the door at home, and greeted my parents, the first thing my father said to me was, 'Doesn't he talk funny!' I thought the same about him, as I had been with the Aussies and New Zealanders for so long I almost felt I was one of them.

When I went to bed, I couldn't sleep as the bed was so soft, and I had to get out and sleep on the floor.

It was a shock to find that things at home were going on as if I had never been away, many still in reserved occupations making plenty of money and keeping the best jobs.

Whilst we had nothing from our government to go back to, I have since heard that the German POWs had a free gift of 12,000 marks, plus 12,000 on loan, and also a pension, and they were given a medal. It makes one wonder who won the war.

I was terribly thin and very yellow when I arrived back home, but my health soon picked up as we were allotted double rations for six weeks.

After a few days, who should turn up but Slim and his pals. This was more of a disaster than a reunion, as they proceeded to paint the town red. Girls were flocking from everywhere to meet them as they looked very dashing in their big hats and new uniforms, not forgetting the large amount of back pay they received, and spent like water. Their government had given them all their back pay in one lump sum, which they proceeded to make fly as quickly as possible. They used to count out all their money on the bed, and all the coppers they got rid of to anyone passing, saying 'We can't carry that lot around!' In fact they gaily spent all their money, and I remember I had to give them some of mine to help them get back to their Camp, which was a long distance away.

I found them accommodation in an inn in the town, and when I visited them there I found the bedroom full of girls. They certainly enjoyed themselves, and who could blame them. My parents could never get used to my Aussie pals calling for me at home and shouting out 'Where's that Pommie Bastard!' They were quite disgusted. After a day out with the boys I always returned home drunk and very merry, though never violent. The lads also 'fixed me up' with a widow (much older than myself) which I wasn't very pleased about, and neither were my parents, who were very shocked. In fact, they spent most of the time while I was home in a state of shocked disbelief.

I took one young lady into their bedroom at the Inn, and her father, who was a butcher in the town, came after me with a knife! I didn't continue that acquaintance! People were not so broad-minded in those days as they are today and always presumed the worst.

My parents were very sniffy about my friends and hoped they would soon go back to Australia. The people I had left behind had no idea whatsoever what we had all been through and certainly did not seem very interested. We were just nuisances who interrupted their own placid routine.

One night, the Aussies and myself went to a dance in the local town hall and nearly caused a riot, as the Aussies kept their hats on when they were dancing. The MC told them it was not allowed on the dance floor and they must remove them. Naturally they took not the slightest notice of what he said, and when the MC insisted and was getting egged on by the British forces there, I could see a fight brewing. I rushed up to the MC and told him to forget it, or the place would be wrecked. There is nothing more ferocious than an Aussie, who has been cooped up for four years, without his hat.

After our six weeks' leave, we were all called back to our respective camps, and that was the last I ever saw or heard of my Aussie friends. I did write to an address given me, but never got any reply or knew if they had received my letters.

I was ultimately demobbed from Bordon Camp in Hampshire but just before that Fate took another hand in my life. I met the Cornish lady who had spent the war years inspecting Spitfires and married her, and I am still happily married after 47 years.

I had determined never again to live in the Black Country after seeing so much scenic beauty in Austria and luckily, with my wife's help, we came to live in the beautiful county of Cornwall.

I have recorded these experiences at the request of my wife who thought they were interesting, sometimes tragic and sometimes amusing, and she has helped me to write this book.

After all these years memories come flooding back of the

pals made in the war years and, as with so many older people, these experiences are clear in my mind. The worse one's circumstances are, the more valued is the comradeship.